T0324355

Integrity

For Nick, John, Stephen and Tom

Integrity

The Rise of a Distinctive Western Idea and Its Destiny

MARTIN ALBROW

polity

First published in 2025 by Polity Press

Polity Press
65 Bridge Street
Cambridge CB2 1UR, UK

Polity Press
111 River Street
Hoboken, NJ 07030, USA

ISBN-13: 978-1-5095-5986-2

A catalogue record for this book is available from the British Library.

Library of Congress Control Number: 2024938579

Typeset in 11 on 14pt Warnock Pro
by Cheshire Typesetting Ltd, Cuddington, Cheshire
Printed and bound in Great Britain by CPI Group (UK) Ltd, Croydon

The publisher has used its best endeavours to ensure that the URLs for external websites referred to in this book are correct and active at the time of going to press. However, the publisher has no responsibility for the websites and can make no guarantee that a site will remain live or that the content is or will remain appropriate.

Every effort has been made to trace all copyright holders, but if any have been overlooked the publisher will be pleased to include any necessary credits in any subsequent reprint or edition.

For further information on Polity, visit our website:
politybooks.com

Contents

Acknowledgements

My work on the theme of integrity began at the turn of the century, while a Fellow at the Woodrow Wilson Center in Washington, DC. I was fascinated by the righteous indignation of the American public electing a president to restore 'honor and integrity to the White House'. The State University of New York at Stony Brook was generous in its welcome soon after, and I am grateful for the resulting friendship of Wolf and Anahi Schafer and the ideas they gladly shared.

While in the United States, I met former British diplomat Graham Leicester, who shared my interest in integrity and invited me to work with his International Futures Foundation, newly founded in Scotland. My warmest thanks to him and all his colleagues at that time, in particular Anthony Hodgson and Andrew Lyon, who each in their own way stimulated my early thinking.

Subsequently, as a visiting fellow at the London School of Economics' sadly disbanded Centre for the Study of Global Governance, led by Mary Kaldor and the late David Held, I enjoyed and remain grateful for our discussions on integrity with scholars there, especially Helmut Anheier, Olaf Corry, Marlies Glasius, Hakan Seckinelgin, Sabine Selchow and

Geoffrey Pleyers (giving me the chance to congratulate him on recently becoming president of the International Sociological Association).

Later in 2013, I was resident fellow at the Centre for Advanced Studies in Law and Culture at the University of Bonn, where Werner Gephart and Daniel Witte were ever ready to follow, and sometimes save, my lines of thought. I thank them and Marta Bucholc of the University of Warsaw, also a fellow in Bonn, for their friendship and interest in my work. Other scholars with whom I have enjoyed both friendship over the long term and many fruitful exchanges while preparing this book include Anthony Giddens, Stephen Kalberg, Ino Rossi, Sam Whimster and Joy Zhang. Please accept my immense gratitude for the continuing pleasure of talking and thinking with you.

Materially, this book is the recent product of frequent discussions with a few people. My friend Colin Bradford, non-resident Senior Fellow of the Brookings Institution, has been a constant source of advice over the last twenty years. Zhang Xiaoying of the Beijing Foreign Studies University gave me my initial insights and Xiangqun Chang of the Global China Academy provided subsequent feedback on Chinese thinking around integrity issues. My warmest thanks to all three.

Above all, Hugh Canham, author and former managing partner of the city law firm Denton Hall, has at one time or another read, though not necessarily approved, every word of this text. This is the kind of generosity that only old school chums can experience. We have been in it for the long run. I'll continue to be immensely grateful to him, as we both are to our mutual boyhood friend Barry Amond for the occasional, but much valued, words of support from Australia.

'Retirement' has allowed me the freedom that even the most accommodating employer cannot provide, and I have been blessed with the love and continuing encouragement from my wife Sue Owen, who has ungrudgingly supported my travels, figuratively and actually, to the places and topics I find compelling. Occasionally and to its benefit, she has cast her eagle eye over the text. Without her, this book could not have been written.

It is an added pleasure to have this opportunity to thank our tech entrepreneur son, Thomas Albrow-Owen, who has provided essential guidance on things atomic and subatomic.

I will not embarrass John Thompson with the single word that would summarize the completeness and high standards he requires and derives from the synergies of being publisher, professor and scholar at one and the same time. It is enough to thank him warmly for the multiple occasions of feedback and advice he has given to help me bring the ideas in this book to a wider reading public. For his colleagues at Polity Press, too, my warm appreciation for your professional work. My thanks in particular to Gail Ferguson who has made copy-editing a fine art form.

London, April 2024

Preface

It's an extraordinary story. Integrity! The word that began with the honour of the virgin girl in ancient Rome is now the guarantee for fair elections in the West in 2024. We see it – and we don't see it – everywhere.

Over two millennia, integrity has been a quality mark for the distinctive contribution of a few western countries to making the world modern. It's a quirk of history that a single word mirrors so much of the expansion of the West. But then so much of history is a random walk through the past.

The origin of the word was the Latin '*integritas*'.[1] It entered everyday language towards the end of the Middle Ages, signalling extremes, like the power of a woman or a resource for the cunning ruler. For integrity can apply to almost anything, or *any thing*.

Integrity points to distinct things, separate from others, complete in themselves. But it also means having high standards, especially moral, but also material, like being durable. For integrity applies to natural objects as well as human beings, and to the things they make.

The combination of those two meanings, to form what Lewis Carroll called a portmanteau word, is unique to the languages with that Latin origin. Those countries speaking them happen also to be ones that built the empires of the West – Spain, Portugal, France and Britain.

They also happened to be Christian, inheriting the belief in a God who had made all things. When the idea of completeness and standards was subordinated to a belief in the creator God, integrity became a religious requirement. Later, in the sixteenth-century Reformation in Europe, when the Catholic Church lost its exclusive hold on believers, the rebel Protestants could seek to emulate God's creativity.

The United States inherited all those cultures and took integrity into new territory. It became the calling card for its founding fathers and the stern instruction for its young people. Integrity inspires individuals to excel. To this day, it coexists in frequent tension with integration into churches, communities or organizations. Integrity and integration: both words that evoke different aspects of existence.

This is one reason for the longevity of the word – it applies to whatever exists. But the other reason is the linkage with standards. For that expresses the greatest discovery of all, the recognition of what makes us human, namely that our existence involves both material and ideal dimensions or, as it used to be expressed, the material and the spiritual. All cultures recognize both spheres of reality, but only these languages of western imperialism have a single word to cover both.

Now it would be gross to suggest that the word has driven the history of the West. But it has accompanied it, and developed over the centuries, to reflect the changes that it has experienced. Some of its power and hold over the imagination is a relic of its origin. For the Romans, the physical basis of virginity was equally moral, and the sexual connotations of integrity remain sufficient to bring down national and corporate leaders to this day.

But, as this book seeks to show, the scope of integrity has expanded vastly over the centuries. On this very day (literally as I write), there are at least two quite different references to integrity cited in the press. In one case, the European Commission is planning guidelines to counter threats to the integrity of elections that are likely to affect X, TikTok and other online platforms.

The other reference is to the long-running saga of the Rupert Murdoch media empire and victims of phone hacking, who are extending their allegations to implicate journalists and other employees. News Group Newspapers are quoted as saying that this is a 'scurrilous and cynical attack on the integrity of those named in the case'.[2]

On the one hand, integrity refers to an institutional and familiar feature of contemporary life, namely elections, on the other, to the moral and professional standards of professional people. We don't feel any incongruity there, and should we be scientists we would not be surprised to read about the integrity of soundwaves.[3]

So, what can't have integrity attributed to it? That's more difficult because integrity is part of the fabric of everyday life, and absence calls out for attention. But for some things we have no expectation of integrity – the weather, for instance, where we have no control, and which has no obvious boundaries. It is hardly a 'thing' or a distinct entity, however much it has an impact on us.

Human beings following their interests to the exclusion of all else have no integrity. In that case, morality is an external restraint on them. Consequently, as we will see in this book, markets inherently have no integrity except that which is imposed on them by legislators and regulators. All of which results, in capitalist systems particularly, in much effort being expended to get round the rules that authorities have imposed.

In the following pages, I trace the course of integrity from the ancient world through to the present when every culture has access to the idea in a globalized world. It is the West's gift to the rest, even as it has lost its centre and, in my terms, unwound, distributing the results of its efforts far and wide.

Simultaneously, we also need to attend to the alternative worldview that has pervaded non-western cultures and persists to this day. For them, the world is a seamless web of relations, and things are inherently bonded with each other. Our global future depends on the cooperation of both views of human existence, a world of relations and a world of things.

1

An Ancient Legacy for the West

The idea of the West has taken plenty of knocks in recent years. Speculation about a decline of the West is at least over a century old.[1] That, in one respect, explains why I have written this book. For me, the West has dispersed or, in the word I use later, unwound. Its influence remains global, even if its core is in pieces. But that is some way ahead in my story.

Rather than this being a history of the West, I am going to follow an idea that is essentially western, and in so many ways an indicator of its basic impetus and motivations. It crops up in every sector of life, usually without comment since it is so familiar. But that is why integrity deserves closer attention because it comes near to what has been at the heart of the West for two millennia and now expresses so much of its present crisis.

This chapter will trace the meaning of integrity back to its origin in the Latin word *integritas* and take us forward to the beginning of the modern period by which time it had acquired most of the scope it has today. And behind *integritas* there is *integer*, with an original meaning of whole and intact, surviving as an English word to this day, meaning a whole number.

Whole numbers make it easy to count things, and the idea of integrity starts off with objects or entities that are separate from each other. But then, and here is its secret power, it adds another aspect, intimacy with standards or values of all kinds, material, moral, intellectual or aesthetic. In that connection with standards, it survives as an entity and seeks to fashion the world around it, call it context, environment or culture. At one time, for some even now, this would have been called its spirit.

This is the secret of integrity. The bonding of values and standards to the idea of wholeness, of the complete entity, creates a concept that is unique in the West. It mirrors and expresses the special drivers behind the West's expansion. It is a continual impetus towards invention and exploration. It provides the creativity momentum of the West.

For those of us in the West, like me, the peculiarity of integrity is not immediately obvious. It is only when we begin to translate it into other languages that it becomes apparent. Not so with Spanish, French, Italian and Portuguese, for they all preserve a near replica of the original Latin. Along with the English, and with their shared offspring, the United States, they spearheaded the worldwide expansion of what we call 'the West'.

With all their national differences, they have the same dualistic idea of integrity. Their integrity is restless and always incomplete. For when completeness is bracketed with standards and fulfilment of values, there is always room for improvement. Perfection is never achieved in the search for integrity, even if advances may always be measured.

When we move outside the Latinate languages to German for instance, *Integrität* is a rarely used loan word dating from the nineteenth century. The nearest equivalent, *Rechtschaffenheit*, conveys correctness, observance of standards but not the complete entity. It is often translated, however, as integrity.[2]

But take a Celtic language like Welsh and there is no equivalent. It has never used integrity as a loan word. The *Welsh Academy English–Welsh Dictionary* translates integrity as *gonestrwydd, cywirdeb* or *uniondeb.* Those terms in the *Dictionary of the Welsh Language* are rendered as honesty or truthfulness for *gonestrwydd*, rightness or correctness for *cywirdeb* and straightness or directness for *uniondeb.* None of these convey the duality of the English word.[3]

So it is in the rest of the world. Travelling further afield, the translation of the word 'integrity' into Chinese poses the same problems that any non-Latinate language faces. While the meaning of completeness or wholeness can be translated '完整' [wan zheng], the moral aspects appear as '正直' [zheng zhi] (uprightness) and '诚实' [cheng shi] (honesty), and at other times are translated as '诚信' [cheng xin] (good faith), or '操守' [cao shou] (moral principle).[4]

Reflections on existence

The absence of a word for integrity is only a minor aspect of a profound difference between Chinese culture and the West. Integrity as a concept expresses the separateness of things, even as they embody or reach out to principles. In Chinese thought, things are bonded into the seamless web of reality, *tianxia*, all under heaven.

In classical China, the sage Lao Zi (born 571 BC) interpreted the ancient wisdom of the Dao De Ching where the idea of Dao is of existence composed of ever contending and combining opposites in an infinite reality. Often translated as 'the way', it covers both human behaviour and natural objects. The world-famous yin/yang sign symbolizes the unity and interplay of those opposites.

There was a time in the West when similar ideas were represented by the Greek philosopher Heraclitus (535–475 BCE). He explored how the many might have arisen out of the one, how the world was a fundamental unity, but composed of opposites, in permanent tension, always in flux. 'It is not possible to step into the same river twice' was one of his typical ways of expressing ceaseless movement.

Modern science reflects, too, on the fundamental nature of reality. Fritjof Capra has drawn our attention to the similarities between the worldviews of Heraclitus and Lao Zi. Further, he has argued that modern physics' discovery of ever deepening complex relationships of subatomic particles is consistent with these ancient senses of the unity of existence.[5]

However, a fateful intervention occurred to disrupt this fundamental consensus between eastern and ancient thought in Europe. This was the development of atomism in the century after Heraclitus. Linked also with the names of Democritus and Epicurus, reality is no longer a unity. It now consists of distinct units, atoms, each indivisible but separate from each other in space. They are in constant motion and, when they collide, they create new things.

It is difficult to overestimate the long-term significance of this innovative line of thinking for the development of the distinctive civilizational characteristics of the West and its unique features compared with the East. Thus, the great historian of Chinese science, Joseph Needham, pointed out that atomism played no role in its traditional practices.[6]

For a twentieth-century writer on the history of philosophy, Bertrand Russell, atomism resembled modern science more than any other ancient theory.[7] It refused to look for ultimate causes, to ask why, and simply sought to answer how something happened. It was a mechanistic outlook, suited to the much later development of experimental science, pulling things apart, seeing how they worked.

Atomism was a fateful step, followed by many others that led to increasing separation from the wisdom of the East.[8] It shifted attention to a world of things in which human beings were exposed to events they did not control. Things, moving independently of each other in unpredictable ways, made an environment of ever-present threats. Actions to ward off those threats become an equally important imperative.

It is a deep-seated feature of dominant western ways of thinking about the world that has persisted to the present day. How do we as human beings come to terms with a world we have not made and where we are simply one set of entities, among many others, all with their own distinct place in creation? Even the most prominent critics of the Epicureans, the Stoics, aimed mainly to provide an alternative code of behaviour for human beings in a very similar world.

The world of entities becomes especially alarming in times of uncertainty. For the ancient Greeks and Romans, the philosophy of Epicurus both provided some reassurance and also inspired one of the greatest literary achievements of all time, the *De Rerum Naturae*, 'On the Nature of Things', written by the Roman aristocrat Lucretius (*c.* 99–55 BC) in the century before the birth of Jesus Christ.[9]

In a poem of more than 70,000 words, Lucretius ranged over the need for peace to the atomic constitution of matter, over the mind and spirit to the finality of death, over the existence of deities to their absence from human affairs. He asserted that all entities in the world had their own properties and therefore the freedom to have special effects on others. Those qualities inhering in the entity would make distinctive contributions to the course of future events.

Lucretius explored the human condition. He began from the very foundations of existence, and no aspect of human behaviour was off limits for his imagination. Integrity is the common feature that human beings share with natural entities, the quality of being an identifiable whole object.[10]

It alludes to the very existential nature of the person and to the place he or she occupies in the whole of creation, and at the same time it points to the distinctive feature of the place of any entity whatsoever. In the case of the individual human being, the place is known as society, embedded in nature and framed by culture.

In one of his most celebrated, if notorious, speculations, Lucretius asserted that the smallest possible constituent of matter, the atom, and the human being shared a common characteristic, namely free will. Though often derided because he declared that both swerved and collided as they moved, it was his basic assumption that the atom and the person were similar in this respect. They each shared the same attributes that governed their behaviour.

It was a contemporary of Lucretius, the celebrated Roman orator Cicero (106–43 BC), who has provided posterity with the fullest use of integrity. Through his engagement in political disputes, Cicero is the classic source for the language of public debate in his time. His uses of *integritas* covered meanings of undamaged, soundness of mind, incorruptibility, chastity and purity of language.

The Latin root of *integritas*, namely *integer*, conveys the underlying sense of unity and continues to be used to this day for the single undivided numerical value. But there is no moral sense involved. The contrary was the case for its derivative. With long-term consequences for public discourse in the West to this day, *integritas* went beyond wholeness to cover value-laden ideas of moral perfection.[11]

The association of ideas that brought completeness together with morality in the Latin was female virginity. The sexist assumption in the public morality of the Roman Republic was that a broken hymen meant loss of virtue, the end of chastity.

This linkage of the physical and the moral is the root of the duality of meaning in integrity, retained to this day in all the languages that have a word derived from the Latin *integritas*. It was to have the long-standing consequences for public discourse that became one of the distinguishing features of western culture.

We may infer from the incendiary power of the word 'integrity' in public debate that some of those original sexual connotations are buried not far below the surface. We will find them amply illustrated in Shakespeare, even with geopolitical connotations!

An archetype at work in the Roman imagination lurks behind the western consciousness. Bill Clinton's misdemeanours with a young woman weighed much more with the American public than the history of the dubious business dealings of the Bush presidents' forebears.

If today we see integrity as an issue in every sector of life, it is because, like Lucretius, we appreciate the unbroken chain of being that links us to the existence of the universe. Beyond that, at the same time, we feel our contemporary troubles threaten the unique position that we have created for ourselves in the world around us.

We shall find in our exploration of the idea of integrity that the concerns the poet Lucretius addressed in his epic poem, namely the nature of existence and the variety of things in the world, remain to this day as the deep and underlying direction to which all references to integrity take us. Call it pathos, call it hubris, the culture of narcissism or what you will, it is our frequent reference to integrity in every sphere of life, human and natural, that has made it into the watchword for the special crisis of our time.

Integrity in early Christian thought

The hold that integrity was to take on the western imagination was established during the long domination of Roman Catholic Christianity. The only language that enabled the warring princes of medieval Europe to find an accommodation between their competing interests was Latin, and this was essentially the preserve of those educated in religious schools and universities.

What concerns us here is the twist that Latin authors gave to the idea of wholeness by linking it to moral virtue. The early texts of the first three centuries after Cicero tended to equate the word with sexual purity. Christian writers gave particular emphasis to its association with chastity. But virginity, too, was adopted into Christian narrative with the idea of the Blessed Virgin Mary, mother of God.

Margaret E. Mohrmann, a professor of both religious studies and medical ethics, has traced how early Christian writers were primarily concerned in their discussions of *integritas* with what God had in mind by creating girls as virgins.[12] The raising of the discussion to a higher level came about by considering integrity as purity rather than simply an unbroken hymen.

It is with the writings of Ambrose of Milan (339–397) that a change can be detected. More emphasis was placed upon the moral achievement of chastity rather than the preservation of physical virginity. In fact, the idea of integrity now applied to the whole person, male and female, possibly a reflection of Ambrose's reading of Cicero in particular.[13]

In the thirteenth century, the most influential Catholic theologian of the later Middle Ages, Thomas Aquinas (1225–1274), revived the original Latin dual emphasis in *integritas*, wholeness plus morality. In the lives of saints, it meant striving to reach further to achieve a spiritual state of being. Aquinas claimed moral purity belonged to Adam and Eve in the Garden of Eden. Through their mortal sin, they lost their original *integritas*. But believers in the Christian God could recover that state of sinless perfection by taking the Church's sacrament of penance.[14]

It was its infinite scope of integrity that Aquinas envisaged in his most all-embracing reference to its wholeness, namely to the universe. He argued it was the duty of a king to secure the continuity in official positions, just as divine providence ensured renewal of corruptible things through generations 'and so conserves the integrity of the universe' *(ut vel conservetur integritas universi)*.[15]

The early citations in the *Oxford English Dictionary* (*OED*) come from the fifteenth and sixteenth centuries and are overwhelmingly from Christian contexts.[16] They come under three main definitions:

1 'The condition of having no part or element taken away or wanting; undivided or unbroken state; material wholeness, completeness, entirety.' Its first citation is from Sir Thomas More's *Workes* ('The answere to the first parte of the poisoned booke' 1533): 'not y sacrifice nor oblacion, whyche to the integritie thereof requyreth both the forms.'

2 'The condition of being not being marred or violated; unimpaired or uncorrupted condition; original perfect state; soundness.' Its citation from 1450 speaks of Christ's birth 'savying his moders integritee'.[17]

3 'In moral sense' 'a. Unimpaired moral state; freedom from moral corruption; innocence, sinlessness'. The first reference in 1561 is from the English version of the reformer Calvin's *Institutes* and speaks of man finding eternal life through integrity 'b. Soundness of moral principle; the character of uncorrupted virtue, esp. in relation to truth and fair dealing; uprightness, honesty sincerity.'[18]

Strikingly, the *OED* reference make it clear that the original combination of meaning that the Latin *integritas* carried survived into its reception in English printed texts in the fifteenth and sixteenth centuries.[19] It left open the possibility of revisiting the complete separation of the two sides of the moral and the material that was always implicit in the original Latin. It was to be a direction that was followed ever more vigorously in the following centuries. For a time, the Christian world held them together, but it was not to last.

Tracing the development of the Christian idea of integrity through to the English King James version of the Bible of 1611, 'integrity' appears several times, but no longer is the primary emphasis on chastity. Now it is being used as the translation for terms like *innocentia* (blamelessness) and *simplicitas* (guilelessness), which appear in the original Latin version of the Bible, rather than *integritas*.

For those who held true to Christian principles, integrity became a matter of a way of life, and the Psalms of the New English Bible intoned:

> Judge me. O Lord, for I have walked in mine integrity . . .
>   (Ps. 26:1 repeated in 26:11);
> Better is the poor that walketh in his integrity, than he is that
>   is perverse in his lips and is a fool (Pr. 19:1);
> The just man walketh in his integrity . . . (Pr. 20:7).[20]

Mohrmann sums up Christian integrity as denoting not simply wholeness and completeness but also reliability over time, the predictability and visibility of goodness in a person who was consistently just and honest.[21] This elaboration of the core meaning of the Christian idea of integrity through the Middle Ages highlights the contrast with the ambiguities that we shall see mound up to surround it in later periods.[22]

It is difficult to overestimate the importance of Christianity for the development of the western idea of integrity. In its essence, it underpinned the Epicurean view of a world of things. But it was the emphasis on the supreme position of God as their creator that set the West off on a course that was eventually to overwhelm all other civilizations. The very first sentence of the King James Bible runs: 'In the beginning God created the heaven and earth,' and the first chapter of the first book, Genesis, is a recitation of the comprehensiveness of his creativity, from 'great whales and every living creature that moveth'.

That linkage of a world of things with the idea of divine creation was a conceptual legacy for the West long after Christianity ceased to control everyday life. The Christianization of atomism brought the idea of the creator God to bear on the self-image of the human being as well as on the origin of objects. The elements had now been assembled to make the quest for integrity a key factor in western development.

Writing in the 1960s, the French historian Fernand Braudel, widely acknowledged among professional historians of the time as pre-eminent in their trade, was able to write that Christianity was 'an essential reality in western life' even for atheists.[23] 'Western Christianity was and remains the main constituent element in European thought – including rationalist thought, which although it attacked Christianity was also derivative from it.'[24]

The expansion of the West

What we now regularly call 'the West' has developed over the last two millennia from an amalgam of the heritage of ancient Europe and the Christian religion. Accompanying its expansion into the Americas and growth into a wider world empire, it adopted the idea of modernity as its special quality.

With modernization as its mission, and with its extension as globalization, the West has crossed the boundaries of every other civilization. In respect of China, for instance, it engages with a civilization with the longest continuous roots stretching back in time, having sustained its distinctive culture through centuries of contact with others. The continuity of a civilization is also associated with the meanings it attaches to its own place in a wider world, and of human beings within it. In its culture are embedded existential assumptions about human life and death, other living beings, the environment, the past and the future.

The aim of this book is to show that integrity has developed in conjunction with these themes as a distinctive feature of the western outlook on life. In its reference to the wholeness of any entity, and the dependence of an entity on the observance of principles, integrity is the counterpart to the fluidity and transient nature of so much of western life. It also reaches into its continuous drive for innovation. We can call it a central meme, an idea reproduced over time and repeatedly in different contexts.

From its beginnings in ancient Rome, integrity has taken hold in the languages that are derived from Latin. They also happen to be the languages of the peoples who voyaged out of Europe into the Americas and around the world. Spanish, Portuguese, Italian, French and English all adapted the word to their respective vernaculars. It accompanied the restlessness and striving of all the colonial nations.

Other ideas too lasted the course from ancient origins through to the expansion of Europe in the sixteenth century, with the voyages to the American continents and around the world. One was, of course, 'empire', which cropped up repeatedly in the intervening centuries as an image of transnational order and control.

Integrity emphasized morality. But if you put it together with empire, then, as we shall see in subsequent chapters, it provided a potent combination to fire up the imperialism of later centuries. Integrity became the great counterfactual, the quality forever eluding the seeker after perfection, always escaping the hold of those who imagine they have it in their grasp.

When the times are chaotic, when the individual is in deep trouble, integrity is the repeated appeal for a halt to the damage, the destination that promises safety and stability. When peace and contentment can offer lasting satisfaction, then the restless imaginations of the explorer or the artist, the inventor or the prophet find alternatives to a settled existence and invite others to cross boundaries into new worlds.

Integrity is a watchword and signal of an outlook in the peculiar civilization that the West has thrust on the rest of the world. It is also a condition, never permanent, of both the natural world and the things we make, and sometimes of ourselves, from time to time. In recent times, globalization has been the shorthand term for all such features that make up the distinctive quality of the age we have been living in, the restlessness, the new frontiers, the dangers for so much that is held dear. In that context, seen in the light of its original framing, the reader can appreciate how integrity has come to represent the contrary counterpart, expressing opposition to what otherwise seems to threaten to sweep away all that is familiar and cherished.

With that in mind, we will continue to follow integrity in this book from its origin in the Roman Republic to see if in any way its past holds out hope for repairing the precarious state of our world today.[25]

2

Integrity Becomes Modern

There are many ways to date the beginning of the modern age. But there is general agreement about the cumulative effect of a whole series of events in Europe from the fifteenth century onwards. There was the reception of technologies originating from the most powerful of regimes of the time, China: the compass (for voyages), gunpowder (for entertainment and killing) and printing (for communication), all fuelling subsequent western expansion.

But more significant than technology was a change of mindset, the emancipation of thought from the control of the Church. The discovery that the Earth revolved around the sun and not the reverse shook religious hegemony over ideas. Equally, the recovery of many ancient Greek and Roman texts inspired independent thought.

The challenges of new discoveries, the break-up of Western Christendom and the wars that accompanied the religious turmoil had been anticipated by another kind of incursion, namely the rediscovery of pre-Christian ideas in originals or copies of ancient manuscripts. Among fundamental challenges to the Christian worldview was the atomism of the Epicureans, reaching its culmination with the re-emergence of Lucretius.

Long lost, the find in the early fifteenth century of a complete manuscript of Lucretius' *On the Nature of Things* gave great impetus to what became known as the Renaissance. Its atomism, an emphasis on distinct things, served as a basic assumption in the outlook and subsequent development of 'natural philosophy', later known as the natural sciences.[1] Montaigne, the French provincial official, author of the *Essais* (1588) that have left an indelible mark on western literature, quoted from Lucretius almost a hundred times. In turn, Shakespeare was a great fan of Montaigne.[2]

By the sixteenth century in Western European history, integrity as a concept had become part of public discourse in the vernacular. It was also a period when the established order of things was unsettled in fundamental ways. The Earth might not, after all, be the centre of the universe.

New continents existed to the West, and the authority of the Catholic Church was undermined both intellectually by Protestant dissent and by political apostasy. Religion itself became a political resource for a king of England and Wales like Henry VIII, who could establish a new Church to divorce one wife and take another.

Ultimately, however, it was probably printing more than anything else that acted as the solvent of the old order. It meant the possibility of circulating texts in the vernacular, and with them ideas that did not just depend on biblical authority. The French dictionary *Larousse* dates *integrité* from the early fifteenth century and gives it the dual meaning from the start: on the one hand, something intact or undiminished and, on the other, a person of moral wholeness, incorruptible.[3]

In such a time of political and religious flux, integrity both came into focus and into question. Time and again, its bonding of completeness and values came under stress from the logic of power. It was possible even to ignore the lack of integrity in holders of political power, or indeed, advise them to ignore it. In Italian vernacular, the word was *integrità*, and that acquired lasting notoriety through the work of one man who has been called the founder of modern political science.

Niccolo Machiavelli and the New Realism

A short treatise by an adviser to the Italian princes of the time did more than anything else to highlight the novelty and contradictions then existing and to leave a lasting imprint on the centuries to come. Niccolo Machiavelli (1469–1527) wrote during the Renaissance when artistic glories and brutal inhumanity coexisted in the same urban space.

He himself had laboriously copied Lucretius out by hand.[4] His model prince was Cesare Borgia, employer of Leonardo da Vinci, builder of a canal from the town of Cesena, the same place where Borgia placated the populace by displaying in the public square the body of his hated chief adviser – sawn in half!

Machiavelli's early sixteenth-century treatise, *The Prince* (1513), circulated earlier, but printed first in 1532, survives to this day as the benchmark for modern realist accounts of politics. It stipulated that the love of one's people was the best fortress against enemies from outside. Certainly, that meant keeping faith with them. But then there was a catch.

One of Machiavelli's most famous passages in *The Prince* is in chapter 18. It has the title 'In what way princes must keep faith'.[5] It begins: 'How laudable it is for a prince to keep good faith and live with integrity, and not with astuteness, everyone knows'. But then he goes on to contrast the fox and lion, the one operating by guile, the other by force.

Both methods had to be employed for the purpose of maintaining the state. The prince had to display many qualities. Indeed, 'he should seem to be all faith, all integrity, all humanity and all religion.'[6] But the key word was 'seem'. He continues, 'Everybody sees what you appear to be, few feel what you are.'[7]

Nothing ought to come out of the prince's mouth that was not full of faith, integrity, humanity and especially religion since people could actually see that, and they could be taken in by appearances. But if necessity dictated, then the prince had to be prepared to do the opposite of what those qualities required.

In treating political power purely in terms of success, Machiavelli aligned the prince with the forces of nature and, in this way, with the long-established meaning of integrity's completeness. He could easily have written of an integrity beyond morality. Instead, he chose to treat integrity as the value for ordinary people to cherish and, as a result, capable of being manipulated by holders of power.

There has never been a more succinct statement of the pact with the devil that the ruler of a state makes. That is, if perpetuation of that rule is the overriding object. But the blatant immorality of chapter 18 should not detract from the other purposes of rule. For, once established, it is the basis of the well-being of its subjects, of their security, property and commerce.

The ruler was advised to mingle with his people in the festivals he laid on for their entertainment. And 'nothing does so much honour to a newly risen man than the new laws and measures which he introduces.'[8] But, in a world where good and evil coexisted in full gaze, anyone who dared to take charge of events and create something that would last had to reckon with both sides of reality. A ruler ought to be both feared and loved but, on balance, if a choice was necessary, it was better to be feared.

All was to lead to a new scion of the house of Borgia creating an army that would unite Italy. The vision was to shape the future of a nation. There we can see from our vantage point in a world of nation-states how integrity as wholeness has become the outcome of a creative process. Power is itself the means to making a new entity, and the moral qualities have become instrumental in its creation. Power uses integrity to create an integrity, an entity of wholeness.

In his account of power, the twentieth century's most celebrated advocate of reason as the basis of philosophy, Bertrand Russell, distinguished the 'power to do' from 'power over'.[9] Both are needed in technological civilization. Without power, both over his employees and his algorithms, Mark Zuckerberg could not have created Facebook.

Russell pointed to the chasm between the genius heights and the scoundrel depths of the Renaissance and judged Machiavelli to 'glorify naked power'.[10] But it is difficult to imagine Russell's simple distinction being possible without the brutal clearing of the wilderness of illusion that Machiavelli achieved in one short book of advice for rulers, at a time when he too suffered its excesses along with so many others.

Power is the passage between integrities, the destruction of one and the creation of another, and in the human world the creative process will engage with the standards that guide and lead to the accomplishment, the work of art or the robot. Integrity in both its senses, wholeness and moral worth, combined in the one word in English, will be both means and the target of the power to create, phases in a process that has become an unending upheaval in our lives today.

The seminal influence of Machiavelli on posterity was summed up by Lord Acton, adviser to Prime Minister William Gladstone, a founder of modern historiography, editor of the iconic *Cambridge Modern History* (1902–10) when he wrote: 'He represents more than the spirit of his country and his age ... The authentic interpreter of Machiavelli ... is the whole of later history.'[11] Acton continues: 'He is the earliest conscious and articulate exponent of certain living forces in the present world ... Religion, progressive enlightenment, the perpetual vigilance of public opinion have not reduced his empire, or disproved the justice of his conception of mankind.'[12]

In that world of brutal contrasts, Machiavelli had no difficulty in formulating paradoxes that have both fascinated and repelled generations of students of politics and power to this day. He was one of the early shapers of the discourse of modernity, a common reference point for his successors in that role, Michel de Montaigne and Francis Bacon, while Shakespeare's plays provide lasting evidence of Machiavelli's influence on public life.

Machiavelli's ideas were a frequent source of debate in Shakespeare's time. They provided a fertile ground for the dissemination of non-Christian ideas. These included the atomism of Lucretius. Shakespeare slipped in an incidental reference in *Romeo and Juliet*: A 'team of little atomi' could disturb Romeo's sleep, said his friend Mercutio.[13]

Shakespeare's play with power and integrity

The creative tension between power and integrity gained full exposure in Elizabethan England. Paradoxes spring up like mushrooms in a damp field at dawn: a new Church from a king's adultery; seats of learning funded from promiscuity; the virgin ruler sponsoring slaving voyages. In that context, Shakespeare found plenty of occasions to mention integrity.[14]

The time-honoured allusions to female virtue recur, as in *Love's Labour's Lost* when the Princess of France resists the king Ferdinand of Navarre's invitation to come to his court:

Now, by my maiden honour, yet as pure
As the unsullied lily, I protest,
A world of torments though I should endure,
I would not yield to be your house's guest;
So much I hate a breaking cause to be
Of heavenly oaths, vow'd with integrity.

It was virtue so deeply grounded that a suitor could only 'discover such integrity' through poetry and music as in *The Two Gentlemen of Verona.*

But integrity went beyond women's virtue to be the summation of personal moral qualities in Shakespeare's characters, even when attributing it to themselves, as did the duke in *Measure for Measure*, pledging his 'coat' and 'persuasion' as well as his 'integrity' to convince the doubting Provost of a promise. Status, beliefs and values, we might say today. The duke declares later of another, 'His integrity stands without blemish.'

Clashes between moral fervour and lust for power are explored in depth in Shakespeare's later plays. It is with *Coriolanus*, a play dated around 1608–9, when we come to the first instance of integrity being used in a direct political context. The warrior hero, bearing the name of the play from his victory at Corioli, newly elected consul, challenged the honour of the Roman tribunes. They had voiced the people's accusation that he had despised them for wanting free handouts of corn:

> Your dishonour
> Mangles true judgment, and bereaves the state
> Of that integrity which should become it,
> Not having the power to do the good it would,
> For the ill which doth control it.

The tribunes (of whom one is called, not coincidentally, Brutus) then denounce him as a traitor. Coriolanus is telling them that it is they, the tribunes, who owe the state their integrity to enable it to work for the common good. It is a statement of the necessary bond between the state and its servants that happened to have been both avowed and tested to breaking point in Tudor times.

Under James I, Shakespeare makes it the duty of the crown's servants to withstand democratic forces. Integrity comes into fullest prominence in what was almost Shakespeare's last play, *Henry VIII*, written in collaboration with John Fletcher. This was also high politics, and it begins by telling the audience they are about to hear things 'full of state and woe'. It was advertised as 'the famous history of the life of Henry VIII', but it was only as distant in time from them as the world wars are from us. As we know, all such accounts are highly selective.

Fully two-thirds of the action in *Henry VIII* concerns the power and the fall of the king's mighty servant, his Lord Chancellor Cardinal Wolsey. He was intimately involved in Henry's schemes to be rid of his first wife Katherine. Summoned to appear before the king in court, she makes a fervent plea for justice and his pity, but it is Wolsey who responds, telling her that those 'assembled to plead your cause' are 'of your choice, – these reverend fathers; men of singular integrity and learning, yea, the elect of the land'.

At this, Katherine turns on Wolsey and accuses him of being her 'most malicious foe'. Later, on another occasion, when Wolsey tries to make peace with the now deposed queen, she tells him to speak out, 'truth loves open dealing.' He answers in Latin, '*Tanta est erga te mentis integritas, regina serenissima*' – (such is the integrity of your mind, most serene queen).

There seems to be some double innuendo here since she cannot understand the Latin, and yet in it *integritas* echoes chastity. So she asks for the truth in English, to which Wolsey replies that he is 'sorry my integrity should breed ... – and service to his majesty and you – so deep suspicion.' We may surmise that Wolsey emphasized his high professional status by speaking Latin to provoke the queen into humbling herself, as she did by asking for plain speaking.

When Wolsey fell from the king's favour, he told his faithful secretary, Thomas Cromwell, to take an inventory of all his possessions: give the king his robe, 'And my integrity to heaven is all I dare now call my own'. Tellingly, reflecting the new power relations, later in the play, it is the king who makes integrity depend on himself, ordering Thomas Cranmer, Archbishop of Canterbury, to stand up, 'thy truth and thy integrity are rooted in us, thy friend'.

It was Cranmer who Henry defended at the end, giving courtiers power to put him on trial, but then intervening to accuse them of acting 'more out of malice than integrity'. It was Henry's commission that required their integrity.

Henry VIII was a parable for the time it was written, too, echoing the fall of another lord chancellor, Francis Bacon, and the extensive manoeuvrings of the court of James I. There are more references to integrity (five in all) than in any other Shakespeare play. It is unlikely that the audience would not have grasped the intended message of support for the monarch as the source of legitimacy. They were alert and serious listeners.

But Shakespeare speaks across the centuries. For an archetypical message for our own time, we should turn to his *Cymbeline*, which has all the ingredients of the politics of integrity. Intrigues, deceptions and confusing, ambiguous personal relationships prevail between characters of various nationalities, only for the honour of the main female character, Innogen, to be sustained throughout and for a peace between nations to be achieved.

Cymbeline is a geopolitical drama where integrity is the supreme quality that proves to be the sure defence of virtue and will eventually triumph in an environment of conspiracy and deceit. The players are representative of the national powers. Britain has its king and queen and also the two main characters, the king Cymbeline's daughter Innogen and her husband, not a nobleman, but of impeccable qualities.

Wales provides primitive honesty and strength. Italy is home to a motley collection of characters, good and bad, and also provides Iachimo, who threatens the chastity of Innogen, through his wager with her husband that he can seduce her. Spaniards, Dutch and Frenchmen also get walk-on parts.

Innogen's chastity is beyond virginity. She has a husband. She protects her virtue even in the gravest danger, having to escape the wrath of her father, the king, by adopting a male identity. Even in this elaborate tale of honour maintained through all adversities, even to the end where Innogen's husband is deceived to the point of nearly killing her, Shakespeare conveys the Machiavellian distinction between authentic integrity and integrity merely performed.

In the denouement, Cymbeline learns from a physician, from whom his second wife had purchased poison, that she despised Innogen and only pretended 'to love [her] with such integrity, she did confess was as a scorpion to her sight'. The conclusion of this extraordinarily complex, even contorted plot, finds Cymbeline, though he had defeated the Romans in battle, declaring he would pay his tribute to Caesar and the Roman Empire. 'And in the temple of great Jupiter Our peace we'll ratify, seal it with feasts.'

Shakespeare's message was that the confusion of relationships between human beings, extending even to war, would only be resolved by steadfast virtue. And through that the perpetuation of an empire was assured.

This archetype in the western imagination sets up integrity as the guarantee for a settled world, able to repair any conflict and confusion in it. Its themes echo in the subconscious depths of the public mind to this day, as in the contrast between the integrity narratives of the Bush family and the global rhetoric of Bill Clinton.

In the plays of Shakespeare, integrity has settled into the everyday public discourse. His audiences were aware of a world where new knowledge and new territories broke old boundaries in thought and deed. Power and virtue were in contest in a chaotic present, but better futures could always be imagined.

Integrity was invoked as a sign of deeper bonds between people as moral and political agents. It represented another aspect of the transition from the medieval into modern times that extended to multiple other spheres of life, throughout religion, science and economic activity.

This period of history that modern scholars came to call a rebirth, a Renaissance, opened up a double life, the actual and the imagined. The popularity of dramatic performance reflected a general appreciation that the past could have been different, and the present offered alternatives. Shakespeare's 'All the world's a stage and all the men and women merely players' celebrates options, banal though they may be, that are in any person's repertoire. Dissimulation is not just the privilege of the Prince.

Francis Bacon and the new science

In the career of the eminent, ultimately disgraced Francis Bacon (1561–1626) there was a full parade of the paradoxes of the newly secularized idea of integrity. His contribution to rethinking the place of knowledge and scientific advance in human progress remains a landmark in western thought. In his time, he was also the greatest lawyer of the land.

Bacon emphasized 'faith and integrity' as the obligatory components of being a counsellor to a ruler.[15] As for judges, in his essay 'Of Judicature', he wrote 'Above all things, integrity is their portion and proper virtue.'[16] While holding the position of lord chancellor, the highest law office in the land, he was found guilty of taking bribes. (His subsequent disgrace should be a warning to all who campaign for power by calling for the elimination of corruption!)

Some years after his death, the story was recounted that Bacon died from a chill he caught outdoors. He was supposed to have been checking on the progress of an experiment to see whether snow would be as effective as salt for freezing a chicken! The story fits the person and his reputation, if not the facts.[17]

Bacon's scientific ambitions were even higher than his status as a lawyer. He was a fervent advocate of the new experimentation and measurement, inspired by Copernicus and Galileo, and the discoveries that challenged old religious orthodoxy. He was an avid collector of reports of experiments on everything from plant germination to sedatives.

Indeed, his fame has lived on as the originator of the modern belief in progress, its basis in the advance of science and promise of a better society. His *Advancement of Learning* (1605) turned its back on the medieval scholastic tradition based on Plato and Aristotle and promoted ideas going back to Democritus, seeing how things worked, finding truth from empirical evidence rather than pure reasoning.[18] His posthumous *New Atlantis* (1626) envisaged a fictional society that was guided by scientific research.[19]

Integrity for Bacon was not something that belonged simply to official duties. It was also a quality of character that belonged to friendship too. To treat another 'to work him, or wind him, or govern him, proceedeth from a heart that is double and cloven and not entire and ingenuous; which as in friendship is want of integrity, so towards princes and superiors is want of duty'.[20]

Bacon was the most eloquent and celebrated voice of his day in applauding the advance of science, seeing in it the mark of a new age. His appeals to integrity could not fail to emphasize its links with the pursuit of knowledge and in important respects redress the quite contrary stress in the writing of his infamous predecessor.

The fraught ideal

Machiavelli, Shakespeare and Bacon spoke eloquently for their time, supreme raconteurs of its stories of ambiguity and balance, clarity and confusion, discovery and disruption,

scepticism and conviction. Integrity inhabited their new discourse, no longer the medieval prerequisite for life on this
earth and ever after, but a moral condition that could be both
aspired to and simulated, an ideal, but one that invited pretence and dissimulation.

Machiavelli's ideas became a common property for educated Europeans. Rulers, having made loyalty a foundation for
their rule, were overthrown by those who 'have been able by
astuteness to confuse men's brains'.[21] The same message of
ambivalence towards integrity was still being conveyed two
centuries later by the maverick thinker Bernard Mandeville
(1670–1733). Likened on occasion to Machiavelli, he regarded
evil as the foundation of society, and 'Goodness, Integrity and
a Peaceful Disposition in Rulers' ill-suited to 'Aggrandize'
a nation.[22] 'There is no Innocence or Integrity that can
protect a Man from a thousand Mischiefs that surround
him.'[23]

Of course, supporters of monarchy were also ready to pro-
claim its virtues against such Machiavellian accounts. The Tory
Viscount Bolingbroke (1678–1751) wrote his essays applauding
rule by a 'patriot king', who would see the 'the orders and
forms of the constitution are restored to their primitive integrity'.[24] Bolingbroke denounced private ambition as producing
division and corruption 'in opposition to union and integrity
of government'.[25] We can see in Bolingbroke's defence of the
monarchy the ever-widening scope of the idea of integrity. It is
a quality belonging, not just to individuals, but to government
as a whole.

The eighteenth century saw integrity occupying an established place in Samuel Johnson's (1709–1784) great *Dictionary
of the English Language*, first published in 1755. It has an extensive entry, with its derivation from the French and Latin, and
lists three meanings: 1. Honesty: uncorrupt mind; purity of
manners; uncorruptedness. 2. Purity; genuine unadulterated
state. 3. Intireness: [sic] unbroken; whole.[26]

Johnson subsequently reflected on integrity in his fable *Rasselas* (1759). He put these words in the mouth of an astronomer: 'Integrity without knowledge is weak and useless, and knowledge without integrity is dangerous and dreadful.'[27] The story was a huge success at the time, and an astronomer's wisdom then was perhaps the persuasive equivalent of what our particle physicists tell us today.

It equally evoked in Johnson a sense of the frailty of life.[28] There is a heartfelt passage in a letter he wrote (19 June 1783) near the end of his life to a very close friend, Mrs Thrale of Streatham in London, that says much about the depth of existential anxiety that integrity can convey: 'I felt a confusion and indistinctness in my head which lasted, I suppose, about half a minute; I was alarmed, and prayed God, that however he might affect my body, he would spare my understanding. This prayer, that I might try the integrity of my faculties, I made in Latin verse.'[29] It would appear from his biographer's account of the great man that integrity also rated for inclusion in his epitaph. James Boswell lauded the sincerity of Johnson's deathbed penitence: 'when we consider his almost unexampled attention to truth, his inflexible integrity, his constant piety, who will dare to "cast a stone at him?"'[30]

By the eighteenth century, integrity occupies an ambiguous place as a necessary ideal that was also dangerous to pursue. That is one possible implication in Johnson's assertion that integrity was useless without knowledge. Recently, some have called that time of early modernity the first period of globalization. They have in mind the territorial expansion of the Western European nations. Equally, the instabilities of today's globalization have their counterpart in the religious upheavals of the sixteenth century.

Those who fled what they saw as an increasingly godless Europe, from the Reformation onwards, began to set up communities in the New World. This was a momentous voyage, not just over the ocean but into territorial space that continually posed new problems of living together and, in turn, new solutions.

The very creation of a new society was built on the dream of making integrity a reality. It inspired the great modern experiment of the whole period, the United States of America. That slippery ideal, the elusive idea of integrity, came to be a hallmark of the modern world.

3

The American Experience

For Adam Smith, author of *The Wealth of Nations* (1776), founder of modern economics, the discovery of America was to be one of 'the two greatest and important events recorded in the history of mankind'.[1] The subsequent reshaping of the relation of individual to society took on fundamentally different features from the medieval village community living under the gaze of God's representative.

Previously in the Middle Ages, the ancient Greek dictum of Aristotle, that human beings are community animals, served as the formula on which the overarching control of the Catholic Church was based. With every fracturing of religious unity, rulers of European states were emboldened to adopt Machiavellian methods, while communities of Protestant believers sought new freedoms.

In the tumultuous changes of the Reformation, the new premise was that free, like-minded individuals set up autonomous communities. American history has been deeply influenced ever since by highlighting every opposition to state control that led to the waves of emigration from Europe. The founding belief of the American way of life is the original freedom of individuals, free to form their own associations. They do so by their free decision.

For their paragon figure for all the personal virtues stemming from this belief, Americans have long looked to Benjamin Franklin (1706–1790). When we explore his moral code, we will also be considering him \as an exemplar of capitalist motivation, just as the German sociologist Max Weber did, but for a rather different reason, namely for innovation as much as for wealth accumulation.[2]

That leads us to consider the longer story of American character formation through to its uneasy incorporation into the theory of community integration in the twentieth century. In the relations between personal integrity and social integration, we shall be exploring the tension that inhabits the American dream and motivates individuals to ever-greater efforts.

Benjamin Franklin as the talisman

Max Weber, long recognized as one of the founders of classical sociology, made Franklin famous for all subsequent generations of students in his classic study *The Protestant Ethic and the Spirit of Capitalism* (1920). Weber chose him to represent the quintessential or in his terms 'ideal type' of a religious ethic that underpinned modern capitalism.

The use Weber made of Franklin was to highlight words of advice he wrote for the 'young tradesman' and for those who 'would be rich'. They included the famous 'time is money'. But credit was also money, and a great deal had to be done to maintain one's credit. Hearing you hammering away at five in the morning reassured a creditor in the way seeing you at the billiard table would not.[3]

The instrumental aspect of Franklin's approach to integrity, and indeed to morality generally, did not escape the notice of the generations that followed him. For Weber, a unique feature of capitalism as it developed in the West was the pursuit of profit as an end in itself, and he portrayed Franklin as the incarnation of western capitalism.

In doing so, Weber himself became an important voice in the western self-image, bringing an increasing polarization between values and science into focus, and celebrating it with his doctrine of the necessity to observe value-freedom in scientific work. At first glance, Weber writes, any German person reading Franklin on the practical uses to which moral behaviour could be put would write it off as typical American hypocrisy. But Weber goes on to correct that impression.

For the underlying assumption behind Franklin's moralizing was ultimately not its utilitarian uses but his belief that making money was an end in itself. It was an 'ethic' that, paradoxically for most people, excluded any possible enjoyment of the fruits of their work. Though, in Weber's terms, 'a bland Deist', Franklin recalled his father quoting to him a proverb from the Bible that a man vigorous in his calling would stand before kings.[4]

Franklin, a founding father of the American Constitution, diplomat, polymath and man of the world, guaranteed integrity's central place in the American belief system. One scholar, Leo Lemay, has attributed to him nothing less than 'the definitive formulation of the American Dream' and described him as 'the most famous man in the western world' in the later eighteenth century.[5]

Franklin wrote in his *Autobiography* (1793) that '*Truth, Sincerity* and *Integrity* in Dealings between Man and Man were of the utmost Importance to the Felicity of Life.'[6] He committed himself to it in his journals and declared himself to be such a man, compiling a list of thirteen virtues that should be observed in the pursuit of his 'bold and arduous Project to arrive at moral Perfection'.[7]

Franklin's ethic was not just a set of maxims for ritual recitation. It expressed a spirit that informed daily life and guided his interventions in public life. Summing up his life to date in 1784, he advised linking Integrity with 'Probity' to say that 'no Qualities were so likely to make a poor Man's Fortune.'[8] He then got himself into a bit of a tangle by claiming that he had learned humility to conquer pride:

> Fifty Years past no one has ever heard a dogmatic Expression escape me. And to the Habit (after my character of Integrity) I think it principally owing, that I had early so much Weight with my Fellow Citizens when I proposed new Institutions or Alterations in the old; and so much Influence in public councils when I became a Member.[9]

Then he goes on to declare that nothing is so difficult to subdue as pride. In the end, he reckoned (in a rare instance of self-deprecation), even when thinking he had completely overcome it, 'I should probably be proud of my Humility'.[10]

This was Franklin's complete list of the virtues, in their original sequence:

1. Temperance
2. Silence
3. Order
4. Resolution
5. Frugality
6. Industry
7. Sincerity
8. Justice
9. Moderation
10. Cleanliness
11. Tranquility
12. Chastity
13. Humility.[11]

The list is the central point of the second part of Franklin's *Autobiography* which he wrote while staying on in Paris, having been chief negotiator for the United States in the Treaty of Paris between the United States and Great Britain which ended the American Revolutionary War in 1783.

What concerns us here is the position of integrity, or rather its lack of position. *It is absent from the list of virtues.* We shall see this often in the rest of this book. Integrity is not itself a virtue. It is much more; it is a container for them, extending its reach far and wide across every virtue.

Franklin links integrity with 'truth and sincerity', and then again with 'probity'. Only sincerity figures in the list of virtues, and that makes a special connection between truth and the person: whoever speaks the truth must believe it applies to the speaker too. Arguably, 'probity' is precisely the combination of truth and sincerity. In other words, integrity brings with it, in addition to any one or all of the virtues, a gathering up of the person with them. It conveys a comprehensiveness and completeness beyond them all, an embodiment of their potential. It is not just another virtue; rather, it accompanies each one of them and becomes the impetus behind the complete set.

A whole line of the founders of the United States joined in Franklin's enthusiasm for integrity, citing it as a core component of the qualities essential to the citizens of the new republic. George Washington wrote to his cousin in the middle of the Revolutionary War to ask him as 'a person in whose integrity I have not a doubt' to make sure that he disbursed the usual charity that the Mount Vernon estate gave to the poor.[12] The third president of the United States, Thomas Jefferson, advised his nephew that, after improving his mind with science, then the highest esteem would be gained in following the interests of country, friends and himself 'with the purest integrity, the most chaste honour'.[13] Later, writing to Founding Father Benjamin Rush in 1808, he ranked four 'qualities of mind': (1) good humour; (2) integrity; (3) industry; (4) science.[14]

Rush himself, writing to John Adams, declared 'integrity in the conduct of both the living and the dead takes a stronger

hold of the human heart than any other virtue'.[15] James
Madison spoke in the Virginia Ratifying Convention of not
expecting opponents to have the 'most exalted integrity and
sublime virtue'.[16]

In the next century, another of the driving moral agents
in nineteenth-century United States, William Ellery Channing
(1780–1842), became for a generation of successful and high-
minded New Englanders the conscience behind their business
success. Unitarianism, as he preached it from the pulpit, was a
creed, without dogma but with a fervent belief in the mission
of human beings to improve the life of all around them. One of
Channing's discourses on self-denial concluded: 'Did any man
ever mourn that he had impoverished himself by integrity, or
worn out his frame in the service of mankind? Are these the
recollections which harrow the soul and darken and appal the
last hour?'[17]

Channing appealed to the twenty-year-old student Max
Weber, who reported back to his mother that reading him he
found that '*This is the first time* within my memory *that something religious has had a more than objective interest* for me'
(italics in original). For him, Channing had an 'entirely original
and often magnificent view of the nature of religion – which
incidentally is hardly to be called Christian'.[18]

Weber's subsequent confident assessment of Franklin's
emblematic significance for American capitalism was based
not just on his texts. He resumed contact with an old friend
and colleague, Hugo Münsterberg, who had left Heidelberg
to become a professor of psychology in Harvard. He invited
Weber to accompany him to a Congress in St Louis in 1904.

Weber was inspired as a result to write vividly of his first-
hand impressions of the importance of Protestant religious
affiliation for American business practice. In particular, he
came to emphasize the formation of a distinct form of human
association, the sect, the bonding of people in a group, based
not on residence but on common beliefs. The degree to which

such groups were open or closed to outsiders was a critical aspect of their relations with the rest of the world.

This distinction between open and closed association parallels one that is a focus of this chapter. The open society has integrity as a guiding principle; the closed one has integration as its constant goal. In the United States, the tension between them provides much of its inner dynamic.

Forming the American character

The classic description of these fundamental attitudes by the nineteenth-century observer Alexis de Tocqueville (1805–1859) remains a valid account of the prevailing and deepest assumptions in American life to this day: all individuals are free and equal; where they have shared interests, they found a community; and communities are free and equal in a state, which they have founded, and in turn they are one of the states of the United States of America.

His remarkable observational skills also threw light on the contradictions in the lives of the inhabitants of the New World: restlessness in the pursuit of new things, in spite of the wealth they already possessed; praise for equality, yet forming exclusive groups; living for life after death but finding success in this life, the paradox that we saw Max Weber making so much of two generations later.

Concern for the future was the great service that rulers could deliver to the people. The pace of change, 'perpetual fluctuation of fate', and surrounding turmoil all meant governments had to plan and to think of a future in this world, now that religions had ceased to inspire a belief in a life after death.[19]

These features, which I prefer to call the flux of the time, were ones that, in the America de Tocqueville described, were kept at bay by the Supreme Court and its judges. They had to be 'men of education and integrity, qualities necessary for all

magistrates, but must also be statesmen' and able 'to understand the spirit of the age'.[20]

A generation later, the renowned Yale Professor William
Graham Sumner (1840–1910), went back to speak at his old
school in Hartford, Connecticut. He chose as his theme 'integrity in education'.[21] For Sumner, integrity included pursuit of
sound knowledge but also 'real discipline in the use of mental
powers, sterling character, good manners and high breed-
ing'.[22] His core message was that integrity in education was the
'opposite of all sensationalism and humbug'. That meant not
just technical knowledge. It required the integrity intrinsic to
conscientious learning, free from the fads promoted by self-
styled 'educators'.[23]

This meant honesty in the widest sense, 'rectitude of motive
and purpose, completeness and consistency of principle, and
delicacy of responsibility. Truthfulness is the very cornerstone
of character ... which all sound education must inculcate. It
cannot do so, however, unless its personnel and its methods
are all animated by unflinching integrity.'[24]

Keen for innovation, Sumner was simply following in
Franklin's footsteps by regarding integrity as a key strategic
quality for success in life. Integrity in education as character formation was intrinsic to the self-esteem of the families
that dominated New England society in particular. It was
reflected in the impressions of the German immigrant who
welcomed Weber on his visit to the United States in 1904,
Hugo Munsterberg. His substantial tome on his new country
included a chapter on 'aristocratic tendencies'. He described
how his university was governed by seven men in whom 'the
academic community has profound confidence in their integrity and their breadth of view.' Moreover, he adds, 'there is
not one whose family has not been of service to the state of
Massachusetts for seven generations.'[25]

Munsterberg was alluding to the combination of patrician
outlooks, social exclusivity and high-minded commitment to

reform that became a significant factor in American politics in the 1870s and 1880s. Men of that background, known as Mugwumps (a word of Indian origin for head guy), though mainly from Republican families, adopted a holier-than-thou attitude to political parties, aimed to eliminate corruption and to roll back universal male suffrage.[26]

Young men with political aspirations like Theodore Roosevelt, who was also praised for 'his "high character" and integrity', might stick with their traditional Republican allegiance.[27] But many Mugwumps openly canvassed the candidacy of Grover Cleveland for the presidency in 1884, even though he was a Democrat. It was his renown for 'honesty, self-reliance, integrity and commitment to the principles of classical liberalism' that secured their support.[28]

In Munsterberg's allusions to the growth of 'aristocratic' traits in American life, there was an implicit suggestion of a process that was not confined to the New World. What was notable in these formulations was how similar they were to the ones that Sumner had applauded. They both relied very much on ideas that had become equally fashionable in the old countries that so many Americans had left behind. Indeed, the principles that were associated with education and self-reliance were equally celebrated in the British Empire, at first glance an implausible place for integrity to find a home.

For the celebrated colonial administrator of what came to be known as Nigeria, Lord Lugard (1858–1945), integrity was an important ingredient in his theory of the 'dual mandate'. He distinguished the imperial drive to make profits out of the resources of the colonized land from the need to protect the culture and institutions of the native inhabitants. To those ends, there was a need to promote a particular type of education.

Lugard's idea of the right education for colonized people emphasized character rather than intellectual training as opposed to what had been practised in India 'which rated the ability to pass examinations above integrity and good citizenship'. That sort of education was 'a prey to the agitator and the anarchist'. Training character developed 'integrity, self-reliance and a sense of responsibility'.[29]

Linking the training of character to education was a main theme for commentators on the purpose of the so-called 'public schools' that were springing up in the nineteenth century for the sons of a class that ruled an empire. What was true for Britain applied also to the new transatlantic civilization and those aspiring to take charge of American expansion. Character building, rather than the acquisition of knowledge, was what superior people in the new democracy required.

Herbert Spencer and the Anglo-American synthesis

A shared emphasis on integrity reveals something about affinities between the expansion of the British Empire and the founding of the United States. Both represented the ambitions for self-expression and individual development in the discovery of new territories. In each case, the novelty of the new environment prompted self-reliance and the necessity for innovation. At the same time, the integrity of people was invoked for building new entities, institutions and companies.

Sumner was the leading light in feting Englishman Herbert Spencer (1820–1903), the self-educated polymath and most famous public intellectual of the late nineteenth century. The confidence of that time in the advance of civilization and its basis in a scientific understanding of the world found in him its most prominent advocate. A legend in his own day, his views, sought by the great and the good, and the not so good, had a worldwide impact. The emperor of Japan, no less, sought his advice.

Sumner had played a major part in introducing Spencer to the American public and his whistle-stop tour of the States had been a triumph. At his farewell banquet, Sumner spoke of Spencer's 'work on sociology as a grand step in the history of science'.[30] In Spencer's view, 'Progress . . . is not an accident, but a necessity. Instead of civilization being artificial, it is part of nature; all of a piece with the development of the embryo or the unfolding of a flower.'[31] For that all-embracing vision of human development as the culmination of evolution, Spencer devised a formula: 'Evolution is definable as a change from incoherent homogeneity to a coherent heterogeneity, accompanying the dissipation of motion and the integration of matter.'[32] Each of the things in the vast store of entities, from planets to plants, from people to palaces, arose out of a process of integration. Here then was a solution for the abiding discomfort with atomism that the West inherited from the ancient world. In that word 'integration', there was also a special affinity between Spencer's worldview and the conditions that prevailed throughout the expansion of the European settlement of America.

Integrity offered a guiding light for those seeking that future in shifting and confusing times, when known and familiar surroundings remained a competing attraction. Those settled habits and clear boundaries of the present gained their intellectual expression in another Latin derivative from *integer*, namely integration.

An underlying tension between integrity and integration has been a distinctive feature of western history from the birth of modern times. We shall see how it has been both a stress and a driver for so many of its creative minds.

In the formation of states, and then the United States, there was a continual process of bringing often far-flung, sometimes mutually suspicious, communities of settlers together into a broader frame of governance, and then to assimilate the steady flow of new arrivals. Integration became a guiding process and destination in this New World.

Making a unity out of disparate parts defines the ongoing process of integration, while integration is also the outcome of that process, the functioning coordination of the parts of the unitary entity that ensures its continued existence. It is a concept that has an appropriate use in any consideration of what holds things together, whether in the natural or social sciences, in creative work or in everyday life.

It fitted too with another concept that grew in importance in the Enlightenment. The theological idea of the world as a product of divine wisdom, of God's design, was secularized in the Enlightenment in the idea of system. The joining together of parts to make a clock could also be applied to bringing people together. Saint-Simon wrote of the 'industrial system' as a unity of science and human agency.

Spencer captured a mood that inspired both the old and the New World: individualism, free trade and a belief in the natural energies of people, rather than the state, to adapt to new industrial conditions. His message gained a huge following in the United States, helped through its promotion by Sumner.[33]

Perhaps it was that felt affinity that meant Spencer's strident individualism, emphasis on 'struggle for survival' and opposition to state welfare resonated in the American Congress. It also inspired the transatlantic tycoon Andrew Carnegie to write as Spencer was dying: 'Dear Master Teacher, you come to me every day in thought . . . The World jogs on, unconscious of its greatest mind in Brighton lying silently brooding.'[34]

Theorizing social integration

Given the unique history of the formation of the United States, it is not surprising that integration became a favourite concept for historians and social scientists. As one example, we can take the formidable account of American society by Robin M. Williams, Jr.[35] At the very outset, he makes it clear that the issue at the heart of his enquiries is how the very existence of a society can be inferred from the behaviour of so many heterogeneous, often conflicting, groups of millions of individuals.[36]

Williams's book concludes, 540 pages later, with a chapter entitled 'The Integration of American Society'.[37] There he makes a point of contrasting what he calls 'the *factual cohesion* of a social aggregate' from 'the *societal integration* that occurs through shared values and beliefs'.[38]

Mere cohesion, as distinct from integration, brings with it no assumption of a collective identity since it simply depends on individual interests coinciding without significant conflict. It refers mainly to a degree of interdependence without shared beliefs. Williams continues, 'A basic postulate is that the integration of a society can be defined in terms of the sharing of common prescriptions and proscriptions for conduct, belief, valuation.'[39]

Williams is only one of many, but still typical, representatives of American mid-twentieth century thinking about society. Integration around values had already become a pervasive theme in western social thought.[40] Its most prominent advocate was the Harvard Professor of Social Relations, Talcott Parsons who merged integration theory with advances in thinking on systems. His tome *The Social System* (1951) was for many years the definitive statement for orthodox sociological theory.[41]

Risking a travesty of a vast and hugely influential list of publications spanning more than thirty years, we can say Parsons's essential argument was that individuals were brought up or trained to occupy roles that fitted the survival requirements of a wider social system. That system was one of human action, organized through institutions according to the famous AGIL scheme of functions: *adaptation* to external conditions; attainment of *goals*; *integration* of individuals into the collectivity; *latency*, or expression of feeling and tensions.[42] Particular social systems were constituted by the 'institutional integration of motivation'.[43]

Institutions themselves for Parsons represented the solution to perpetual dilemmas in choosing courses of action. There were five such dilemmas for any modern institution: affectivity vs affective neutrality; self-orientation vs collectivity orientation; universalism vs particularism; ascription vs achievement; diffuseness vs specificity. Choices between them defined the nature of the social system.

Just as an example of how they worked, we can ask how students should be chosen for higher education. Do we accept any who pass an examination, or do we restrict entry to our own nationals (universal vs particular)? Shall we take account of social class or ethnicity as well as examination grades (ascription as well as achievement)?

It was the entirety of the workings of the whole system that concerned Parsons, but he was also aware of its potential fragility. People's personalities, cultural values and social relationships all needed to be bonded together in 'threefold reciprocal integration' for a society to maintain itself.[44] That integration depended, among other things, especially upon a 'paramount value system'.[45]

These were the features of a particular kind of system, a *social* system. He then defined a society as 'the type of social system that contains within itself all the essential prerequisites for its maintenance as a self-subsistent system'.[46] Inside this system, individuals came and went, by birth, deaths or migration, but they were integrated into socially recognized roles by a general moral consensus governing the system as a whole. 'Every social system is a functioning entity.'[47]

Nothing should detract from the immense and comprehensive theoretical achievement in Parsons's work. It combined old thinking about community together with the latest trends in the systems theories that were sweeping through public and private organizations. It underpinned much of the confidence that the United States had in liberal democracy, and what it felt was its necessary worldwide expansion in the development of post-colonial states.

But, in one respect, the very success of this model of the integrated social system, as it spread throughout the West and beyond, also increasingly illuminated a self-contradictory weakness in a theory to fit New World conditions. These were determined, in the new jargon of the times, and in American eyes especially, by globalization.

The great paradox was that globalization actually illustrated the porous and even fragile nature of the national societies of the day. Emerging multilateral institutions provided the basis for transnational social relations. The advance of computing technology boosted the relevance of networks. Free trade, telephones, not to mention Hollywood, penetrated parts of the world where people had not even learned to read. In this flux, individuals negotiated differing, often conflicting, self-identities, rather than adapting to predetermined social roles. Quite apart from this growing mismatch between the structural functional theory of social integration and the changing world around it, there was a direct ideological confrontation with largely Marxist-inspired thought. There was the obvious long-standing objection to liberal democracy, that it only masked and suppressed a fundamental class conflict between owners of capital and workers that was international and not confined to the boundaries of nation-states. In this sense, Marx had already in the nineteenth century defined what was later called globalization.

The other objection from the left was more idealist than materialist. It pointed to the way Parsons and his followers treated values primarily as sources of internal group solidarity, rather than as opening new horizons to their adherents. Should there arise conflicts around values, and that is normal in society, then for the structural functionalists they were treated in terms of deviance from a dominant consensus, not as intimations of new kinds of society.

Expressing and going beyond all those objections, the Parsons synthesis provoked a strident backlash from radical critics of western society, arguing that the emphasis on shared values minimized class conflict in particular and imputed unity to society where it did not exist.

Those heated debates of the 1960s and 1970s in themselves illustrated the limitations of integration around values as an adequate concept for grounding the unity of social entities. Having the same values as others could just as well produce conflict between their adherents. The drive for integrity itself could motivate people to come together for a common purpose, but equally could create deep divides with others. Not for nothing is territorial integrity to be protected, even as far as the declaration of war.

While European in their origin, the distinctive features of what has become known as the West long ago came to be spearheaded by the descendants of the intrepid voyagers to the New World. They brought with them the willingness to break from the old and create a completely new society. But they brought with them an inner tension that has driven the West ever since. It is the beating heart of its expansion and has multiple expressions. The Weberian scholar Stephen Kalberg pointed to one in the 2012 presidential campaign, 'an overarching dividing line' between the shared community and individual self-reliance.[48] Communitarianism versus individualism is yet another way of expressing this.

Another polarity, radical innovation combined with an insistence on moral cohesion. Those two original motivational drivers continue to exist in constant tension in American society. They are another of the paired opposites, like those we saw above in Parsons's theories, so often depicted as dilemmas.

We should add integration versus integrity to the list. For while both share a Latin root in *integer* that even now survives as a word in English, their direction of travel is quite different.

Integration brings things together but aims for the stable point in time and place. Integrity involves the continuing struggle to maintain identity in the pursuit of higher goals.

Integration is about conformity, working to plan. Integrity is about conscience, finding directions through standards. The balance between the two shifts continually and is evident in the restlessness that is inherent in modernity. But it is the beating pulse of the energy that has driven the West to its present place in the world. Its strength is currently being tested to its limits in the integrity crises of our time.

4

The Elusiveness of Personal Integrity

Individual energy and community formation continued to coexist in creative tension in twentieth-century America. Each had its own dynamic and, through the century, personal integrity came to be ever more contentious as its boundaries were explored.

Even Benjamin Franklin was not immune to criticism from his fellow countryman Edgar Allan Poe and from the Englishman D. H. Lawrence. We will follow the repeated attempts to resolve the contradictions between the individual and the community that they highlighted.

Psychoanalysis was one such attempt, culminating in the utopian reflections of Erich Fromm, when the Second World War threatened all that the West cherished, both individual freedom and settled community. After 1945, the release from the discipline of a country at war was followed by the outburst of self-expression in the Beatnik generation.

Integrity as such was stretched to cover the extremes of individual behaviour and then was subtly displaced on to the performance of self by Chicago sociologist Erving Goffman. If Machiavelli had required pretence and a show of personal integrity, now the performance acquired its own integrity, irrespective of the actor's personal qualities.

From seeing how integrity developed from an idea that appeared to offer a stable point of reference, we will be faced by something both more pervasive and elusive in an ever more fluid and confused world. Full of paradoxes, it will hold out the hope of completeness to anyone aspiring to it, but always avoids becoming a permanent and inalienable part of the possessor's existence.

This is the enduring feature of integrity and the secret of its power. By combining completeness with standards that have potentially limitless scope, it is always reaching out for new frontiers and then progressing beyond them.

'The darkness filled with organs'

We saw in chapter 3 that Benjamin Franklin has enjoyed iconic status in the story of the making of the American character. But diversity and dissent have always been equal partners in the making of American culture. Franklin's *Autobiography* was even parodied by Edgar Allan Poe in a short story, 'The Business Man'. Carrying the epigraph 'Method is the soul of business', it implicitly criticized Franklin for a neglect of soul.[1] In this tale of a rake's progress, Poe had his anti-hero say, 'My strict integrity, economy and rigorous business habits, here again came into play.'[2]

Franklin's outlook could even be the target of vitriolic criticism from outside American culture. English iconoclast D. H. Lawrence parodied Franklin's list of thirteen virtues, that 'bold and arduous Project to arrive at moral Perfection',[3] Lawrence called them a 'barbed wire fence . . . which he trotted inside like a grey nag in a paddock'.[4] Hence, while for Franklin 'Sincerity' meant, 'Use no hurtful deceit, think innocently and justly, and if you speak, speak accordingly', Lawrence substituted, 'To be sincere is to remember that I am I, and that the other man is not me.'[5] Franklin's 'Silence', 'Speak not but what may benefit others or yourself; avoid trifling conversation,' became for Lawrence, 'Be still when you have nothing to say; when genuine passion moves you, say what you've got to say, and say it hot.'[6] Lawrence's remark introducing his version of Franklin's creed is only one of his milder comments: 'I am a moral animal. But I am not a moral machine. I don't work with a little set of handles or levers.'[7]

It was the confected nature of Franklin's project, the artificial canopy he erected above the hidden, even unknown ground of the real impulses and feelings that drive the human being that attracted a similar sceptical response from two very different people, Poe and Lawrence. The two aspects, the moral and spiritual, existed in an uncomfortable relation with the physical and material, within the person as much as in society at large.

That unknown ground of real impulses, what Maurice Merleau-Ponty was later to call 'the darkness filled with organs', was explored in its own peculiar way by psychoanalysis.[8] Freud, the medical practitioner, sought to align apparently random and disconnected personal traits with bodily experience. The philosophy of integrating the person provides the unwritten code for much of the work of mind healing to this day. Melanie Klein (1882–1960), inspirer of British child therapy, saw it as a process of integrating split-off parts of the self.[9]

Analysis shares that same drive for integration that Herbert Spencer had seen as the impetus behind evolution, and which provides the standard for successful systems of any kind. Varieties of integration and the links between integrated entities mark out the hierarchy of holons in Arthur Koestler's synoptic view of human organization.[10] Integration may then easily be equated with integrity, as it is for instance for Jeremy Griffith, biologist and visionary, who aims to put 'integrativeness' at the centre of human striving to overcome alienation from our environment and ourselves.[11]

But however compelling this account of the absorption of integrity into the advance of integration may be, there is still something that remains, over and beyond the absorption of conflicts or adaptation to a world outside. There is no provision for the limitations of integration in human affairs or for the active engagement of human beings in creating new things.

We can find an intimation of those issues in the work of the dissident psychologist Erich Fromm, advocate of a humanistic psychoanalysis. Power, exerted over and separating us from nature, also distorts our relations with each other. Love is the only way to reunite us with the world. '*Love is union* with somebody, or something, outside oneself, *under the condition of retaining the separateness and integrity of one's own self*' (Fromm's emphasis).[12] Union with the outside is something other than adaptation, and it gives integrity a changing identity.

Fromm had previously written a book that became a sacred text for the post-war young generation, *The Fear of Freedom* (1942), where he elevated spontaneous activity to be the realization of self. 'Only those qualities that result from our spontaneous activity give strength to the self and thereby form the basis of its integrity.'[13] This is the affirmation of the unique identity of each and every one of us.

Written as it was in the darkest period of the Second World War, when the triumph of fascism was a real possibility, Fromm did not shirk the dilemma that confronted the integrated self: 'We may have to sacrifice our physical self in order to assert the integrity of our spiritual self.'[14] The difference between his view of integrity and the orthodox view of integration is emphasized by his explicit statement of his disagreement with Freud whose 'essential principle is to look upon man as an entity, a closed system, endowed by nature with certain physiologically conditioned drives . . .'[15]

Fromm continues: 'in our opinion, the fundamental approach to human personality is the understanding of man's relation to the world, to others, to nature, to himself.'[16] In this emphasis, he acknowledged the cultures of the East, especially India, and also the Bible as in 'Love thy neighbour as thyself'. It was the central theme of his bestselling book, still a classic, *The Art of Loving* (1957). The biblical idea, he wrote, 'implies that respect for one's own integrity and uniqueness, love for and understanding of one's own self, cannot be separated from respect and love and understanding for another individual.'[17]

The background to Fromm's stress on the avoidance of loneliness and the need to belong was the rise of fascism and the need for cooperation and non-authoritarian democracy. He was close to breaking open the cocoon of integration without escaping its cover completely. The new society would allow for the diversity of culture, but within it there would be a dominant social character harnessing individual energy to the social system. This would seem to be a strong negative incentive to exercise the positive freedom that his spontaneous individual is afraid to exercise.

In our understanding of this apparent restriction on the individuality and spontaneity that Fromm valued so much, we need to recognize the circumstances colouring his account, where the breakdown of society in the 1930s led to escapes that he describes: sadomasochistic authoritarianism, destructiveness and the automatization of character.

In contrast, for him, 'Firstly, from the standpoint of a functioning society, one can call a person normal or healthy if he is able to fulfil the social role he is to take in that given society.'[18] He could scarcely be faulted for failing to anticipate the luxuries of freedom that his latter-day disciples, the rebels of the 1960s, came to enjoy. If they considered themselves to have a role at all, it was to denounce the society into which they had been born.

Spontaneity is not adequate to capture the relationship between the individual and the world, and certainly misleading if it has to fit the frame or a role. The realization of self comes through making a difference in the world. In that respect, no one can deny that the West has accordingly made its mark! The world continues to live with the consequences.

Drop-out integrity

After the Second World War, after rejoicing, taking breath, reconstructing and looking for a new start, the generation in the West that had won the war experienced a nasty shock. Its young people often showed no interest in their parents' sacrifices. Instead, they began a lengthy party. It culminated when a spirit of revolution engulfed the universities of the West in 1968, making it reminiscent of the year over a century before that marked a similar break between the generations.

That year was 1848. The discontents of young radicals in European states spilled over into widespread rebellions against the existing order, and yet resulted in little immediate change except to encourage future reformers. Similarly, 1968 saw the expression of a mood that was to entrench liberal outlooks in the next generation of politicians. But it did little to change the direction of the main focus of its anger, the Vietnam War, that didn't end until 1975.

Those of the older generation who could sympathize with the discontent of the younger were frequently, like Tom Driberg, politician, leftist and sexually unorthodox.[19] Poet Stephen Spender (1909-1995) had experienced the radical dissidence of the 1930s, as well as enjoying the intellectual and social exclusivity of its literary circles. Spender could admire the integrity of the Bloomsbury writers,[20] but equally he found the same quality in the American Beatniks, who rejected bourgeois morality and aspired to a new social order enshrining participation and spontaneity. As in 1848, it was a revolution of mood without a programme. It was a mood that gained strength from its use of a new medium of communication, television, allowing mass viewing of staged events and exotic costumes.

Beatniks could shock their elders, visually in real time, and yet, wrote Spender, who manifestly sympathized with their nonconformity, 'they did so without self-consciousness or loss of integrity.'[21]

He himself had experienced the crossfire of the generations when he learned that the influential intellectual magazine he had co-founded, *Encounter*, had indirectly, from its beginning in 1953, received funds from the American CIA (Central Intelligence Agency). He felt obliged to distance himself from what he called a 'cynical government operation' and resigned from its editorship in 1967.[22]

The staging of protest is a public event, and even more so in the lens of television. But the Beatniks were deliberately provocative, insisting, Spender said, on parading an outrageous private life publicly on the screen. He was particularly struck by that juxtaposition of public and private with their guru, the poet Allen Ginsberg (1926–1997), who spoke in private of ideas and poetry like a religious mystic. Yet, when he took part in a television discussion with him, he switched straight into a promotional mode. Many years later in 1968, Ginsberg struck Spender as a latter-day prophet, delivering ancient wisdom with the new technology.

A striving for integrity was something that Spender's American contemporary Paul Goodman (1911–1972) also regarded as a characteristic of the Beat generation. Like Spender, he had met Ginsberg, regarding him as 'one of their best spokesmen' and expressing some relief that at least he gasped at the Grand Canyon and paid homage to Walt Whitman, rather than aping Zen Buddhists.[23] But Goodman was mainly concerned to provide a rational explanation for what the majority of Americans considered the ungrateful self-indulgence of the post-war young generation. Integrity for Goodman was a quality shown in the determination of the self-employed to make something of themselves, especially if they had a special talent. 'Stubborn integrity', he called it.[24] He applauded the integrity of the conscientious objector in time of war.[25] While he did not share the Beats' enthusiasm for Zen Buddhism, he commended Daoism to them since it was 'a faith for the voluntary poor, for it teaches us to get something from the act of wresting a living with independent integrity'.[26]

Goodman's book *Growing up Absurd* (1960) regarded both the conformity of the organization man and the rebelliousness of those 'on the road' as symptoms of the same spiritual emptiness. Indeed, he argued that both were in their different ways obsessional conformists. In a review of the book that the Beat generation often regarded as their sacred text, Jack Kerouac's *On the Road* (1957), Goodman only found 'the woeful emptiness of running away from even loneliness and vague discontent'.[27] 'There is not much difference between the fellows "on the road" and the "organization men" – they frequently exchange places.'[28]

Finding a position beyond the identities characteristic of a particular culture at a certain point in time requires anyone to look for abiding features of the human condition. In Goodman's case, his iconoclasm extended to breathing life into a notion that had become unfashionable and even discredited among the social scientists of that period, namely the idea of human nature.

Goodman rejected the notion that human beings were simply a blank sheet on which their culture had a free hand to write anything. There was such a thing as human nature, and cultures that sought to shape it in ways that were inconsistent with it would suffer the consequences, as in: 'If the husband is running the rat race for the organized system, there is not much father for the children.'[29] Implied – they might grow up absurd.

The result of invoking human nature was to question the received categories that social scientists employed to *avoid* discussing it. Goodman considered two such examples in the concepts of role and identity. Parodying the stock idea of role as the expected behaviour for a particular social position, he defined it as 'playing it cool and knowing the technique for a token performance'.[30]

The organization man, a concept made popular by William H. Whyte in his book of that name, could equally be the hipster, one who proved he could do any job and move on.[31] Goodman substitutes 'the organized system' for the organization. As for identity, he aligned it with self-discovery: 'One discovers, fights for and appoints oneself to one's identity. Identity is defined by its task, mission, product.'[32]

The reader in the 2020s may find that over-individualistic, compared with later notions of identity that stress identification with gender or ethnicity or a social group, whether conservative or radical. But the point to be made here is that Goodman was issuing an invitation to think beyond the fashionable jargon of the time, to take account of the individuality of the full person.

He could have gone much further had he been concerned to write a theoretical account of what it is to be human (Hannah Arendt's *The Human Condition* [1958]) had been out for two years). But that was precisely the direction he was determined to avoid. There were in any case many other influential concepts entrenched in social science that provided a particular slant on the person.

One celebrated example we shall meet later in this chapter, associated with the early twentieth-century pre-eminent school of sociology in Chicago, was George Herbert Mead's idea of the self, based in an account of how it originates in social interaction.[33] That has the merit of being closer to the body, the child learning selfhood through the early physical care from the adult, but at the same time it links selfhood so closely to the responses of others that the possibility of growth in autonomous experience almost vanishes from view.[34]

This partial perspective on the individual is of course not limited to social scientists. We only have to think of the limitations of the economist's idea of the rational actor. But we shouldn't be too hard on scientists, social, psychological or even biological, if we find that the human being is parcelled up into their professional boxes. That is their job, yet, once the scientists' object of study has been dissected, the parts can never be reassembled as the whole person.

Goodman did not seek to pursue that impossible task. For him, human nature revealed itself if it was allowed to do so and in ways that could not be pre-programmed. He imagined society organized in such a way that the creativity of the individual person could express itself, and society had to allow itself to be surprised by the result. That distinct and individual wholeness of the person, which is what we can discern in his idea of integrity, could be known in the results of his or her being and doing.

It is not often that the blurb of a book expresses outrage. But the publisher could evidently see the sales value of the first comment they printed on its back cover: 'Mr Goodman is terrifying. Utopians usually are when we take them (or they take themselves) seriously. And Goodman is all the more terrifying because he is a rational Utopian . . .'[35]

By that presumably was meant he had command of the latest academic theories even as he turned his back on them. His early death as well as his anarchist reputation deprived him, and his concern for integrity, of the lasting influence he deserved. It was left to integrity to continue as a concept incidental to mainstream social scientific accounts of the human being without commanding a central place in them.

Stephen Spender admired integrity whether it was in the aestheticism of Virginia Woolf or in the outrageousness of the Beatniks. In the same period of time, when he was admiring the young rebels of America, he met the revolutionary students of the Paris Sorbonne. He described an event in its grand amphitheatre where he and the author Mary McCarthy were on a platform facing an 'immense, shouting, moving, gesticulating

mass' of several hundred students waiting to hear Jean-Paul
Sartre. Addressing them, he transformed the occasion into 'an
attentive seminar . . . a warm recognition of Sartre's best qualities, his integrity, his inability to compromise, his warmth.' He
had, Spender reflected, 'a warm heart and a cold brain'.[36]

Just as with his other references to integrity, he doesn't elaborate on its qualities. Sartre's warmth and an uncompromising
nature are no more intrinsic to it than the beards and incoher-
ence of the Beatniks. Woolf's 'artistic integrity' presumably did
not always involve telling young authors (as she did with him)
to scrap their novels, and we learn no more about it. Spender
freely tags integrity on people, but in doing so reveals no more
of its contents than does a label on a suitcase.

In another context, in his autobiography, integrity appears
to be consistent with severe contradictions in a person's character. Spender writes of an old friend from his Oxford days
whose personal qualities are sacrificed to political exigency,
to the extent even that the 'worst private qualities' turn into
'politically correct public ones'. And yet this person 'was consistent and courageous and his behaviour certainly shows no
lack of integrity'.[37]

This old friend had once been 'Tristram', but, having joined
the Communist Party, became 'Bill'. On Spender's account,
the very contradictions he noted in his friend's behaviour he
experienced himself during his own short membership of the
Party, to which he afterwards reacted with an intense period of
writing poetry, exploring the 'condition of the isolated self as
the universal condition of all existence'.[38]

We can infer then that for Spender integrity implied a
uniqueness of personal existence that was threatened by public
involvement and was correspondingly in his own public and
private experience a matter of fraught concern. This is borne
out in his son Matthew's biography of him with the comment,
'Whenever my father thought his integrity was under threat,
he'd lash out in self-defence.'[39] The younger Spender thought

his father had learned it at school, but it is equally telling that the occasion for the comment was also connected with his father's involvement in the Communist Party. How the Party regarded him meant 'his own view of himself as an honest and upright man was under siege'.[40]

Spender's own sensitivity on integrity and the diversity of the people to whom he attaches the quality provide a vivid illustration of the way it casts a cloak over individuality while celebrating the person it covers. Which makes the qualities of integrity all the more interesting. Apparently, we might find integrity anywhere and still be none the wiser about its qualities. It could be any kind of person who displays it, but we might need to search for a long time before anyone is able and prepared to elaborate on its nature. Since it seems to apply to all types, we are encouraged to look far afield in the remotest places.

Outrageous integrity

Judging someone's integrity is a risky business. Whether the judgement is negative or positive, there is more than a suspicion of self-righteousness, even arrogance. When it concerns someone who has just died, then perhaps an element of generosity is allowed. That could have been the case with John Betjeman, writing to a new widow: 'I find myself constantly thinking of the old thing, and his crotchetiness and his tremendous integrity and humility and, lucky old thing, faith.'[41] Betjeman, middle England's favourite poet, demanding respect for the merely respectable, was hardly the person to applaud outrageous contempt for everyday morality. Yet it is entirely possible to make out a case that he was doing exactly that.

The deceased was none other than Tom Driberg, Anglo-Catholic, former Communist Party member, the original William Hickey gossip columnist for the *Daily Express*, and then Labour MP, even becoming chairman of the Party and at the end a member of the House of Lords. The remarkable extent of his double life (or perhaps multiple lives) could only be revealed in his posthumous autobiography *Ruling Passions*.[42]

The ruling passion was homosexuality, a compulsive motive that Driberg enjoyed to the full, from his schooldays onwards, before and after its legalization. Prominence in public life was no deterrent. In his own words: 'If anything I became more promiscuous after my election to Parliament, relying on my new status to get me out of tight corners.'[43] This he would do by a combination of threats and enticements.

He was friends with the Soviet spy Guy Burgess. That led to him, too, being denounced as a spy, though without any solid evidence. But the point was his whole lifestyle, which was common knowledge in establishment circles, and his roller-coaster career reeked of causes for suspicion. Yet he rode above it all, becoming Baron Bradwell of Bradwell juxta Mare, Essex, in 1976, before dying a few months later.

Before a letter and a visit to Driberg's widow, Betjeman had already added a verse to an earlier birthday tribute he had written:

> The first and last Lord Bradwell is to me
> The norm of socialist integrity.[44]

Of course, irony was only a lesser one of the poet's many skills, but he would hardly normally have written to a new widow in the same vein. Though there was an incidental and probably unintended irony. The relationship between Driberg and his wife was, to put it mildly, less than happy or conventional. It amounted to, in the words of his biographer, Francis Wheen, 'this cancerous marriage, in spluttering recrimination and unremitting cruelty'.[45]

Other opinions of Driberg were beyond scathing. Psychiatrist Anthony Storr called him 'evil', Evelyn Waugh 'satanic'.[46]

But historian A. J. P. Taylor, asked if he had ever known a good man, said Tom Driberg was.[47] At his funeral, it was Betjeman who read the lesson, and the famous Anglican churchman Canon Mervyn Stockwood preached.

The ambivalence of the British establishment was on full display, as was Driberg's attitude to it in his funeral request, that the service should include a catalogue of his vices. His friend, the Reverend Gerard Irvine, vicar of St Matthews, Westminster, duly obliged.

We can view Driberg's life from many vantage points: as a case study of English sexual hypocrisy; as an exposé of the contradictions in the British establishment; how the Christian religion can have an unimaginable capacity to forgive; where British socialism looks down deep into blind alleys (or, in Driberg's case, men's toilets). My concern, perhaps sadly, cannot do justice to any of those themes here, or indeed to Driberg's extraordinary life and career, full of contradictions and paradoxes. In those respects, Wheen (1990) does an admirable job. The single paradox we need to notice is that integrity was indeed attributed to him by more than one famous friend.

Extreme cases can highlight the normal, and there can be few cases as extreme as Driberg's. And it seems to go far beyond any conventional idea of morality. In this respect, we need to review the way integrity as an idea has always extended beyond the human and consider human beings as just one thing among all other things that make up reality. We are entities, in a universe of other entities.

Self as performance

Entities are ever forming their existence through absorbing what is outside, integration; or by shaping themselves according to principles, integrity. The tension between integrity and integration even gained its academic expression in the development of rival sociologies.

Integration, the moulding of a new kind of society centred on values, was represented in the sociology of Harvard and Yale, the schools of the New England aristocracy. In the recently founded upstart Chicago University, the artefactual self-creation of the person, arguably the performance of integrity, was represented by what came to be called symbolic interactionism.

With observed behaviour as a starting point (behaviourism had become the new direction in psychology), George Herbert Mead lectured to Chicago students for decades in the first half of the last century, instilling the notion that the self was created in the course of social interaction.[48] The sense of self for the child derived from the behaviour of caring adults towards it. Then later into maturity, the concepts and rules that shaped the behaviour of the socially competent person were conveyed by the wider society.

It was a Canadian sociologist with a PhD from Chicago who made what has to be the culminating statement for the whole interactionist movement. With a striking paradox, Erving Goffman summed up the cultural relativism of his discipline: 'Human nature is not a very human thing. By acquiring it, the person becomes a kind of construct, . . .'[49]

Even when sociologists have not actually denied the existence of something called 'human nature', they have still emphasized their central concern is for the vast variety of ways it is shaped by the different cultures in which it is situated. Yet Goffman insisted on the ever-creative response of individuals to those rules in their interaction with others. The result was an oeuvre of eleven books over twenty years, beginning with the volume that brought him fame far beyond academe, *The Presentation of Self in Everyday Life* (1959). More than any other social scientist in the twentieth century, he squared the circle of simultaneously attracting the general reader and contributing to high-level academic debate.[50]

Notably, Goffman's explorations into the personal strategies required for negotiating interaction and social relations never reached the point of establishing the requirements for individual integrity. This was not because it was an unfamiliar concept to him. He could easily allude to 'the psychological integrity of the individual' since this indicated the set of qualities that psychologists might establish as necessary conditions for participating in social life.[51]

Equally, he could refer to physical integrity in the context of a mental institution. Inmates of what Goffman called total institutions might well feel their personal safety was not guaranteed when physical restraint was a not infrequent occurrence.[52] But psychological or physical integrity were not his concern. The body and its behaviour belonged to the positive sciences of the objective world. His focus was on rules of social interaction and how individuals observed, broke or bent them.

There might be social settings that involved stipulations about integrity. Goffman was relaxed about reporting such expectations: 'Respect for the competence and integrity of the specialist.'[53] 'Service personnel . . . enliven their manner with movements which express proficiency and integrity.'[54] These are remarks incidental to discussing the behaviour that may be appropriate for different types of settings.

But what counts as integrity is not the subject of his inquiry. It is simply one of those things people might have in mind in those situations. It was their behaviour in establishing and performing in those settings that was the main focus of Goffman's attention. Integrity is 'imputed to the performer' by the audience.[55] This applies whether the audience consists of buyers at an auction viewing the auctioneer, or the passengers on a plane on the receiving end of the flight attendant's services.[56]

That terminology of the theatre, 'audience', 'performance', is central to Goffman's own conscious adoption of the position of an objective outside observer of social behaviour. He both begins and rounds off his first book by commenting on his use of the dramaturgical metaphor. 'All the world is a stage', he says, in the sense that the theatre relies on the successful replication of the techniques that are the basis of everyday behaviour – 'successful staging ... involves use of *real* techniques. Those who conduct face-to-face interaction on a theatre's stage must meet the key requirement of real situations ...'[57] Sincerity, the truthful expression of real feeling and intentions, is always undecidable in real life. The person I am talking to, that supposed 'epidermally bounded container', always has the option to conceal and dissemble even when honesty is the rule.[58] That capacity to deceive is put to use in performing recognizable roles in real life when doing a job allows for the intrusion of the personal touch that may or may not reflect the real self. 'Self then is not an entity half-concealed behind events, but a changeable formula for managing oneself during them.'[59]

Although Goffman nowhere cites Machiavelli, we can trace the origins of his perspective on human behaviour back to his notorious predecessor's recommendation that the prince should always give the appearance, rather than the reality, of having integrity. That capacity, which for the prince is a source of his power, belongs in Goffman's hands to any one of us, not just to the ruler of a state. We all have the power to withhold our real intentions and feelings from others.

But what Goffman implicitly does do is to take Machiavelli that one step further. The show of integrity has itself to be convincing, has to elicit the appropriate response from the other person and contribute to the whole nexus of regular, normally expected everyday behaviour. In fact, the performance has to have its own integrity. It is no accident that the term 'role' applies as much to social behaviour generally as it does to the stage.

Therefore, at no point is Goffman willing to give us a clue on how we might validly attribute integrity to a person. Perhaps he comes close to implying it when he writes of performance as opposed to reality in his example of the flight attendant hamming it up with a passenger to suggest a 'nice personality' behind the uniform.

Goffman's 'Self, then, is not an entity half concealed behind events, but a changeable formula for managing oneself during them'.[60] *Frame Analysis* (1975) is one of his last books, and the longest, where he goes out of his way to rule out the possibility of coming close to the human being behind the signs, gestures and expressions that we use to communicate with others. After 575 pages of copious illustrations of this point, it is a surprise to say the least that Goffman feels he has to return to the famous formula that we cited earlier in this chapter: 'I know quite well that back there, there is only "darkness filled with organs."'[61] An entity, like any other!

Emerging relationships

It is when the entities meet that Goffman's accounts are at their most innovative. For instance, he illustrates in his study of public order how it depends on 'civil inattention', accepting that people can just get on with what they are doing irrespective of the gaze of others in their proximity.[62] But it is the content of the integrity that is imputed to others that is outside the scope of his enquiries. This may be taken for granted by a patient under treatment in a hospital, but it is more problematical for the doctor doing the treatment.

That may sound paradoxical at first, but it is precisely in occupations delivering personal services where integrity becomes a matter of professional ethics and central to practical decisions. Particularly when professionals are employed in organizations that deliver services like education, health care and social welfare, there are multiple stakeholders who have an interest in the outcome and expectations of the service giver that may sometimes come into conflict.

In an account of those dilemmas, Paul Halmos explicitly went behind the impressions that Goffman's performers aim to make for their audience, to the underlying principles. He generalizes from the ethical codes of the personal service professions that they are guided by three values: mastery of knowledge and skill; concerned empathy with the client; professional integrity. In all of these, he emphasizes continuous maximization of the value, '"living up to" is not a finite process; the realization of values and ideals is interminable, not unlike the pursuit of the horizon'.[63]

Professional and client have unequal shares in the meaning of their interaction. The integrity of the other is taken for granted by the one receiving the service. For the service giver, integrity is an endless pursuit. It is where integrity on both sides is a reciprocal expectation that we come to the most problematical of all sites for integrity, namely in personal relations between equals.

Anthony Giddens writes that the generalized trust, which civil interaction in public settings depends on, is something Goffman brilliantly analyses, but then moves on beyond him in two books published in 1991 and 1992, by addressing integrity directly. Rather than stay at the level of interaction, he writes in the tradition of a sociology that looks to the creation of meaning between people. At the same time, he treats this as a moving target, where meaning has to be understood in relation to the cultural presuppositions of the time.

Under the broad canopy of what Giddens describes as late modernity, he paints a picture of people having continually to reassess their sense of self-identity as social life is transformed under globalizing conditions. A person's life becomes a narrative of self-development reaching 'personal integrity as the achievement of an authentic self'.[64]

The consequence of this is that integrity, far from being a closed book as with Goffman, becomes intrinsic to the ongoing creative account of the self, and that in turn is realized in relationships with others. These may achieve the 'pure relationship', where personal integrity involves reciprocal trust in each other.[65] But that purity has no long-term guarantee when the world changes and the self changes with it.

For Goffman, the self is always an ongoing reflexive project. Giddens's achievement is to bring that project into the frame of a changing society and to make ongoing engagement with others the source of personal integrity. This leads us to the concerns of the next chapter: the relation of integrity to creativity.

5

Creative Integrity

From the moment a pretence to integrity was recognized as possible, there was an incentive to make a creative effort to realize it. Then the quality of the performance could rate as an example of integrity. The quest for integrity has inspired the effort, and it can be justified by the result. Thereafter, both the creator and the created object occupy the space between mundane reality and transcendent standards and values that we broadly understand to belong to culture. With such a concept of integrity, there is restless dissatisfaction. There is an extra impetus to create something new, of oneself and for the world around us.

This chapter considers examples of the pursuit of integrity in widely varied walks of life. It begins with the existentialist philosopher Jean-Paul Sartre's rejection of a Nobel Prize, T. S. Eliot's rejection of George Orwell's manuscript of *Animal Farm*, and Virginia Woolf's disappointing response to Stephen Spender. These all find their justification in the name of standards beyond the author.

In the nineteenth century, Karl Marx had already indicated his appreciation of those standards in his account of alienation. It affirms the centrality of art in shaping a non-coercive society.

Art is, moreover, at the heart of the creative endeavours that extend to every aspect of human work and play.

Finally in this chapter, in the recognition of a third mode of existence, namely standards operating between the artist and the created work, we are led to reflect on an abiding contrast between West and East. In the West, integrity has largely displaced references to spirit, while they persist in the East to indicate the bonds between created works and the surroundings in which they are embedded.

Society and the creative individual

The Nobel Prize Academy awards prizes in recognition of outstanding achievement to people who do not enter the competition. Jean-Paul Sartre was the superstar of existentialism, the philosophy of personal integrity that captivated young intellectuals in Europe after the Second World War. He refused the offer of the Nobel Prize for Literature in 1964. The Academy awarded it anyway.

Sartre made it known that as a writer he felt he had to be independent of any institution. In any case, in his view, the prize in the past had not equally represented writers of all ideologies and nations. At the banquet, at which he was not present, he was lauded as a central figure for the young generation, and his stand was held to express Ralph Waldo Emerson's dictum: 'Nothing is sacred but the integrity of your own mind.'[1] If Sartre was declaring his own integrity, he was also pointing to the alternative reality that inspires all creative work. After all, 'equality' is the greatest counterfactual of all, always a standard, never achieved in human affairs. At the same time, his statement to the Nobel Academy aligned him with many radicals of his own time.

Artistic aspiration is a struggle always to avoid being dragged into contemporary realities, political or otherwise. Integrity is for ever the slippery lifeline that creativity clings to. But it never guarantees to provide safety. There is an extraordinary example of its precarious nature involving two writers with world renown, actual in the one case, in the future with the other.

This was when one of the most famous rejections of an author's manuscript by a publisher occurred. The poet T. S. Eliot, earning his pennies as a publisher's editor, turned down what later turned out to be the publishing sensation of the twentieth century, George Orwell's *Animal Farm* (1945). Eliot's letter to Orwell was made available along with other significant literary materials by the British Library on its website in May 2016. At the time he wrote it (July 1944), Eliot was one of the directors of the publishers Faber and Faber. Orwell was an established author, but only later of world renown, living off his writing, yet with a reputation as an independent left-wing thinker and well known as the author of *The Road to Wigan Pier* (1937). It could not be a simple brush off. Eliot felt bound to explain the decision. His colleagues agreed that it was 'a distinguished piece of writing . . . the fable very skilfully handled . . . narrative keeps one's interest . . . something very few authors have achieved since Gulliver'.

Jonathan Swift's *Gulliver's Travels* indeed! No less than comparable with one of the great works of western fiction. So what on earth could have been the reason for rejecting it? Two lengthy paragraphs explained: 'we have no conviction . . . that this is the right point of view from which to criticise the political situation at the present time.' But anyone else could publish it if they 'believed in what it stood for'. That was just the second paragraph!

The third engages with the political thrust of the book, declares his Trotskyite view is not convincing and, in fact, 'what was needed (someone might argue) was not more communism but more public-spirited pigs'.

There is a much shorter fourth paragraph which regrets that another publisher will get the chance to publish it and subsequent work. Eliot concludes, 'I have a regard for your work, because it is good writing of fundamental integrity'. There is probably an unintended irony in this since Orwell's standing as a writer was equalled only by his reputation for almost scary integrity.[2]

So, integrity is not enough to get published (a warning to all aspiring writers!). It would seem that it is not just profit that inspires an esteemed publishing firm, as some worldly wise but hopeful author might think. There is a political agenda, too, or, as many might even say, ideals, or others, prejudices.

Novelist Hanif Kureishi commented on what Eliot's views revealed about writers' self-doubts in the *Guardian*.[3] Worrying about what others will think is of no use to a writer, he declares; 'if the writer has some level of integrity, he or she will always do her best work and will eventually discover whether others are indifferent, wildly enthusiastic or something else altogether.' Kureishi imputes integrity to the author, Eliot was commending the writing. We may recall Stephen Spender's rueful comment on Virginia Woolf: 'When she said, "Scrap it!" I had a glimpse of the years during which she had destroyed her own failures.'[4]

The integrity of the artist is sustained by adopting standards that require difficult choices. Her integrity requires vision, determination, honesty, self-discipline, self-awareness and rigorous attention to detail. These are qualities of the person. They are not exclusive to artists. They belong to any worker attending to the imperatives their work imposes. What belongs to the work is a distinct set of standards.

Those imperatives, in the case of writing, painting or indeed any creative work, arise from aesthetic standards, taken in the broadest sense: graphic, literary, sartorial, horticultural or indeed culinary. The integrity of the product, as opposed to the integrity of its creator, depends on its power to interpret, incorporate and develop those standards for the judgement of the wider world.

In so far as the created entity excites admiration and emulation, it occupies a space in other people's lives. It demonstrates its integrity in its power to inspire others to seek to possess it, even to emulate it and share it with others in a similar endeavour. The kind of responsiveness to its power that the work generates will inspire the shared standards of a group, which in turn will be enhanced by its solidarity and consciousness of its distinct standing in the wider society.

Spender wrote of the intense loyalty to each other of the Bloomsbury group around Woolf. Aware of the interdependence of their kind of artistic perfectionism, and the exclusiveness of the group, he could not feel fully part of it, coming to see himself as of a new generation engaged in the terrible events of a later period. On his gravestone he fancied to have inscribed 'Sensibility is not enough.'[5]

Overcoming alienation

Art occupies the intersection of existence and creativity, where the human being realizes those qualities that some have attributed to God, making something new and whole, aiming for perfection where before there was nothing. Art is the human spirit instilling shape and meaning into the mundane conditions of existence, raising it out of the mere satisfaction of daily needs. A work of art brings to reality what in the imagination can be different.

It follows that art is within the capacity of any person and can be developed and demonstrated in everyday activities. Artistic achievement is realized in the art of daily living. The constant return of the aesthetic imagination to influence everyday life is so commonplace as to regularly escape attention, or to be casually noticed as 'style' or 'fashion'. Yet the time, care and attention devoted to the unexceptional tasks of choosing the decor for a room, creating the right effect in a flower garden, finding the shoes that 'go with' the suit, show us exercising aesthetic judgement as a normal, continually repeated aspect of our daily routine. But is this art? Or, put another way, does 'real' art only belong to the artists?

Only when societies have reached a certain level of complexity, when they can support the distinct occupations of artists, does the aesthetic sense become the specialized concern of segregated groups. In their own interests, they may stress the powers of practice and appreciation that they have and that 'ordinary' people lack.

This can be mitigated in a market society where the artist is an independent producer and sells to the discriminating customer, but then aesthetic value will be dominated by money value. As a result, where disposable income is unequally distributed, the tastes of the wealthiest, associating beauty with expensive objects, will detach art from the requirements of everyday living. The distortion of creativity that thus results can be seen by any visitor to the London Saatchi Gallery or reader of the *Financial Times*'s 'How to Spend It' occasional supplement.

In his reflections on the intellectuals of his generation, the historian Noel Annan asked of Woolf and Bloomsbury the same question she posed in her essay, 'Am I a snob?' It arose precisely out of the issue of integrity. For her, he noted, 'the mind, which gave shape to feelings was the ultimate in life and art. The miseries of adolescence and the falsities of public affairs and institutions were as nothing compared to the integrity that demanded you should detect exactly what you felt and should then, having realized what sort of a person you were, live up to it.'[6]

Woolf herself confronted that tension between self-realization and the limited confines of her group and its privileged background in the English upper class. In her writing, she engaged in a microscopic dissection of its manners and morals, with the rest of society as backcloth. The blade of her introspection was thrust deep between its women's status and their personal experience, twisting it to open the wound and allow the deep creative potential of everywoman to flow.

Integrity for Woolf did not stem from disavowing all of one's upbringing and background but by reaching out beyond them, overcoming their limitations to find truths others can share. It was in art that the English upper class came to the self-awareness that allowed it to break its own conventions. In that respect, its women made an asset out of the fact they were excluded from occupations defined as male, and in that way escaped the philistinism of masculinist culture.

Through writing, women could both explore and undermine the niceties of a culture that kept them in subjection. Woolf's friend Vita Sackville-West's novel *The Edwardians* (1930) has a character with an outside observer role declaring, 'If this is Society, God help us, for surely no fraud has ever equalled it.' The fraudulent characteristics of society as depicted there convey its composition as completely arbitrary, yet outsiders were rigorously excluded. All its members could do was to speak confidently and spend money.[7] There were then no creative outcomes, nothing to encourage new standards.

Yet exclusiveness was precisely the charge levelled so often at the circle to which Woolf and Sackville-West belonged. In a way, Edwardian elite society was no different in its basis from any society. Society in itself neither protects nor undermines integrity. It provides only an extensive arena, challenging all who enter to establish their own claim, both to belong but also to be true to themselves. They can animate society for a greater good or use its power for selfish purposes. The choice is theirs.

But it is precisely the tension between the esteem that a privileged group achieves and the sense of its members that this recognition somehow devalues their individual achievements that the young Karl Marx interpreted in his account of the alienation of aesthetic experience. He saw it as arising out of the early division of labour and the unequal distribution of wealth. He imagined a future of free human beings where the aesthetic human being could work with nature to create an environment in accord with the laws of beauty.[8] With that awareness, whether owed to Marx or not, members of exclusive creative groups could feel discomfort and deny the existence of the group altogether.

This was precisely the case with the Bloomsbury group, all the more poignant precisely because the integrity of so many of its reputed members, celebrated people like Virginia Woolf, Roger Fry or Lytton Strachey, was widely applauded. They were British writers, artists and aesthetes on familiar terms with each other, some more, some less famous, before and after the First World War. The economist John Maynard Keynes was counted among them. Frances Partridge, who knew them from working in the bookshop they used, had never come across people 'who set such a high value on rationalism (a word that now raises many eyebrows), integrity and originality'. Yet she wrote, 'they were not a group, but a number of very different individuals.'[9]

One of their number was Clive Bell, the brother-in-law of Virginia Woolf who agreed with that view. In his essay *Old Friends* (1956), he asked whether 'such an entity as "Bloomsbury" existed'. He knew, he wrote, that the two sisters, Virginia and his wife Vanessa, were at the heart of it. 'But did such an entity exist?'[10] He reeled off a list of five other names deemed by others to belong to Bloomsbury that included the author Lytton Strachey, Virginia's husband Leonard Woolf and himself, who made up a circle in Cambridge in 1899. One of them, Thoby Stephen, was the brother of the two sisters, and the group was enlarged when they set up houses in the squares inside the area of Bloomsbury in London. Could these individuals be called a 'group'? asked Bell.

The group, if so it was, was sometimes called 'the Bloomsberries', and the Great War of 1914–18 inevitably dispersed them, only for some to remain or return and to make friendships with others, who, by their very association, became grouped under that same name. Many acquired the Bloomsbury tag in the twenties and thirties through relationships of all kinds, love, marriage, literary, artistic or simply residential, without feeling part of a coherent group, let alone one that required a particular set of beliefs. They might, in any case, be known to the public in their own right, as with Maynard Keynes, or E. M. Forster, or Roger Fry.

Bell vehemently rejected those who found in Bloomsbury a self-interested clique and suggested the possibility in conclusion that it was simply 'a collection of individuals each with his or her own views and likings'.[11] Perhaps he was so emphatic because by the time he was writing he was already 74 and had become even more peremptory with critics of his friends than he had been earlier in his life. In any case, the fact was that much earlier in his life Bell had been far more subtle with the individual/group relation than in the binary opposition he was to set up in his 'old friends' essay. In 1928, he dedicated a short book *Civilization* to his 'dearest Virginia'. He recalled she had been there at its earliest conception: 'You remember, Virginia, we were mostly socialists in those days. We were concerned with the fate of humanity.'[12] It was to have been called 'The New Renaissance'. The First World War put an end to that.

Yet the subsequent Russian Revolution and Italian coup still left Bell with his idea of civilization intact. For Bell, in a civilization reason rules, but it does not require all individuals to think reasonably. He then writes of 'the tendencies of vague *entities* [my emphasis] of societies'.[13] When reason reigns, a sense of values becomes prevalent, a 'stream of civility' which becomes 'a spirit of the age'.[14] When both reason and a good variety of values prevail, then a society has become civilized. All of which prompted Bell to ask how 'an entity so vague as society' can hold such subtle qualities. He answered his own question by writing of societies' civility expressed in manners, customs, conventions, in laws, in social and economic organization and above all in literature, science and art.[15] These depended on the '"civilized nucleus" of a number of human minds'.[16] 'Groups of highly civilized men and women are the disseminators of civility.'[17]

It was that 'nucleus' that so many saw as a fatal flaw, the germ of a self-regarding elite. Bell's later description of Bloomsbury as simply a set of friends clearly helped him to sidestep the criticism of elitism that his own early book had provoked. It may also have reflected the sad and weary disillusion with any kind of collectivism after a war fighting an extreme version in Nazism.

Freedom in culture

We can see that when push came to shove Clive Bell reverted to the old and persistent Anglo-Saxon preference to describe the human world in binary terms: either society or individuals. But his account of civilization did hint at other possibilities. Could it not have been people participating in activities, like literature, art, journalism, publishing, in other words a culture? Isn't the bonding of culture and society regularly called a community?

But it was collective terms that Bell rejected since they were all part of judgements that he resisted, such as Bloomsbury as a group, gang, clique or chapel. He might have written of a network if he had been younger, or of a system if he had been older, but neither way of finding relations between entities would have appealed to him. His individuals were autonomous. Integrity for their persons and their art was something of a regular watchword for them and how they acknowledged each other. They assumed distinctness from their fellow human beings. It followed that the integrity of Bloomsbury could only be escaped entirely through the fate Virginia Woolf chose for herself.[18]

By an odd coincidence, an academic author of the same sur-
name, Harvard professor of sociology Daniel Bell (1919–2011),
took up the same question and refers to Bloomsbury in the
1910s as an example of what he calls the 'great mystery': 'I do
not know any historian or sociologist who is able to explain it,
but at certain times and in certain places, such a coterie, clique,
cenacle somehow comes together, crystallizes, and coalesces
as an entity in this particular way. And this entity becomes an
identity.'[19]

Bell continues to provide other instances of his thinking
on kinds of entity: in Paris or Vienna in the 1920s and Oxford
in the 1930s. He refers then to the Beats and the New Left. In
examining the place of intellectuals in American society, and
in particular Jewish intellectuals between 1935 and 1965, he
argued their coherent formation meant they could be called an
'intelligentsia'.[20]

With these amorphous movements, his reference 'in certain
places' becomes redundant because their exponents disclaimed
any particular place and adopted lifestyles and ways of thinking that were, or at least aimed to be, independent of location.
Indeed, the free-floating nature of social entities is inherent in
the way social relations are maintained over distance. Today
in the digital age, this is ever more self-evident, but it does not
detract from the searching nature of the questions Bell raised.[21]

Once the formation of entities becomes a topic of interest,
then their existence needs no longer be taken for granted. There
need be no assumption of an external all-powerful creative
agency. Their diversity and complexity become immediately
apparent and the subject of close investigation.

We can contrast Marx's perception of the centrality of art
in human experience with Sigmund Freud's puzzlement about
its existence, and his acknowledgement that psychoanalysis
could say little about it, save that it had something to do with
sex. Freud was looking in the wrong place, always intent on
finding that which was inaccessible to common sense. Had he

taken everyday aspirations at their face value, he could have recognized the aesthetic imperative in the shape that human beings give to everyday living. He might have understood the inner requirement to live their lives as coherent but authentic experience, distinctive, but in tune with the times and other people. He could have seen how they resist destructive forces, strive for the exemplary demonstration of vitality and longevity, extending beyond their individual lifespan to build the heritage of families, communities and nations.

In that context, integrity is often invoked. It may be held up as an example either of a challenge to society or as a reinforcement of its demands. As an example of the insistence on challenge, one critic of pop music in 2012, Dorian Lynskey, deplored the way audiences were demanding entertainment rather than art. Serving up what they wanted resulted in 'the merest peep of artistic integrity' being slapped down. 'I grew up', he continued, 'with the idea that artists were meant to be opinionated and adversarial and art was invigorated by conflict.'[22]

The opposite view can equally be entertained. The drive for self-expression may take a very different form from rebellion, yet it is still that tension between the world outside and the creative impulse inside which provides the impetus for art. As just one example of the affirmative contribution of art, we can take Jennifer Williams's London-based Centre for Creative Communities.

For over thirty years, Williams tapped the experience of artists and educators who shared the view that art, through shaping and releasing personal energy and talent, served to illuminate and strengthen community purpose. Those who worked with such a vision in her words 'have a strong grip on concepts of identity and integrity'.[23]

Oscillation between endorsement and rebellion once set the parameters for most sociological discussion of the relations of individual and society. But it requires a special intellectual background and personal experience to be able to make that connection between art, life and integrity in our own time. Today, academic and professional specialization serves too often to undermine the appreciation of the centrality of the aesthetic drive in shaping everyday life.

One person whose career combined the qualities necessary for that appreciation was Charles Madge, a published poet in the 1930s. In the circle around T. S. Eliot, Stephen Spender and Louis MacNeice, he went on to become the joint founder of the path-breaking research enterprise, Mass Observation. Later, he became the first professor of sociology at the University of Birmingham.

In his book *Society in the Mind* (1964), Madge endorsed the early Marx view and looked towards a non-coercive society guided by aesthetic rather than moral considerations.[24] He prefaced his discussion of an aesthetic utopia by pointing to the tension between the social and the un-social self, and how the latter was not to be equated with some kind of Nietzschean superman or economic individualism.

Dispelling what he called 'sociologistic moralism', or the insistence on social control through values, he calls for the realization of freedom through culture, in his terms an 'un-social eidos', where each individual could resist the excessive demand to conform but develop a self that could also have 'attained a degree of public formulation, for example in art, fiction and humour'.[25]

Madge was pointing to the installation of a different space for individuality in human society, not just expressing or challenging accepted forms of living. That space is occupied by the creative individual choosing to shape the future for self and others.

The spirit of integrity

Probably a poet has a better understanding of spirit and its place in the world than most of us. The world is that complete and comprehensive environment that includes human beings as well as nature, past as well as future. It comprises culture and all the products of human ingenuity and imagination. The 'world' in this sense is unlimited, contains anything that might influence us, of which we may or may not be aware. As such, the world is also undifferentiated, being and non-being coexisting, undivided, and the appearance of distinct objects within it a profound mystery.

The poet William Wordsworth for a large part of his life was writing a poem to be published after his death. He once described it as designed to 'convey most of the knowledge of which I am possessed' and 'to give pictures of Nature, Man and Society'.[26] The following famous few lines are an instance of his sense of that mystery:

> Dust as we are, the immortal spirit grows
> Like Harmony in music; there is a dark
> Invisible workmanship that reconciles
> Discordant elements, and makes them move
> In one society.[27]

'Society' here covers the unity and interplay of different parts, a usage of the time that could express much more than just living together. In this case, it is the unity of the person, or, as he goes on to write, 'The calm existence that is mine when I am worthy of myself.'[28] It is a usage that can apply to the inner workings of any complex object and is well suited to our concerns here.

'Immortal spirit' at first suggests an external force, until the phrase 'like Harmony in music' indicates that the immortality is the result of 'invisible workmanship'. The completeness of

the human being then is intimately connected to spirit and the
world and grows over time. That completeness of a being in the
world equates with the wholeness of integrity.

But what does that mean for the world? There are many
who take such things as the world's population pressure on
resources into account when they consider having children.
Morality does extend to ultimate and remote consequences
for the grand design. The world allows us a space and a period
of time, and in that passing moment we shape ourselves and
affect everything around us. We leave our traces, in words and
deeds, on other people and on other things, sometimes far
distant, but always on those in our immediate presence. This
is our spirit still working as the consequences of our being,
extensions of our existence, often visible in its impact in our
lifetimes, more often obscure even to us, eventually disap-
pearing from sight but infinitesimally always present, never
eliminated from the whole of creation.

Such a notion of spirit fills an essential place in the ontology
of being. It is the impression our existence makes, and has
made, on the world around us. Since everything is the consequence of everything that went before, the spirit of any one
person, indeed of any one thing, has a permanent place in the
ongoing creation of the world. This is Wordsworth's 'immortal
spirit'. The impression it makes at the time may have been
insignificant, and its consequences infinitesimal, but in a world
without end it is nonetheless ineradicable.[29]

Objects have spirits too, clearly, since their place in space
and time affects the position of other objects and living beings.
Nothing betrayed the blindness of the modern explorers of far-
flung places more than their disdain for the spirits of foreign
peoples. For what are those spirits but the changing effects of
objects and people on them in their daily lives, and in turn the
influence they exercise on other objects and people?[30]

This everyday experience of the world as expressed in
the vast and sophisticated pre-modern culture of China was

given the name 'universism' by one great western sinologist, J. J. M. de Groot.[31] For the Chinese, it is the Dao, the ways of the world and the human response to it, assimilating the influences or spirits of both into a comprehensive outlook on life.

Within the world, religions like Buddhism and Christianity can occupy their own space, and even the teachings of Confucius, sometimes called the state religion of imperial China, are only a component element of the great overall worldview. To this day, the Chinese benefit from their generous appreciation of spirits. President Xi is very fond of citing the spirit of Chairman Mao or of the Long March to encourage party members in their efforts to rejuvenate China.

The preamble to the official document that announced the Belt and Road Initiative, a development programme that focuses on building an infrastructure network between countries neighbouring China and further afield, makes reference three times to the spirit of the ancient Silk Road in its first two paragraphs.[32]

In a country with an atheistic constitution, it may appear incongruous to foreigners that spirit is invoked so often, but then the problem arises from western understandings of religion and the way historically those belief systems known as religions sought to monopolize the idea of spirit.

We can almost think of integrity and the Mandarin word for spirit, *jing shen* [精神] as equivalent, but there is of course a profound difference between the wider discourses in which they are embedded. The spirit of the Chinese entity is bonded to it, an integral aspect of it, which in turn belongs to all under heaven.[33]

In cultures other than the West, it is the taken-for-granted bonded nature of objects with the world around them that means the questions bound up in the western concept of integrity do not arise as a distinct set of issues. At the same time, the absence of the concept in the rest of the world means there is not the additional spur to inventiveness and quest for novelty that inspires so much of the western momentum in the economy as well as in the arts.

For in the East the numerous qualities of an object sustain its relations with other objects. The material and spiritual exist on the same plane of reality and not in separate spheres. The spirit of the entity spreads its influence far and wide beyond itself and is held in place by all other entities. The western idea of integrity evokes and indeed demands a realm of standards beyond the person or entity but leaves open its content or how it is attained. The entity with integrity ultimately stands alone.

So in translation, when many different qualities of objects in Chinese culture are all translated into English simply as 'integrity', the distinct and various connections of one thing with others are lost. Thus *wan zheng* [完整] which signifies completeness of a country will be rendered as integrity in 'territorial integrity'.[34] Another example comes with the twelve socialist values. One of them, *cheng xin* [诚信], best rendered in English by 'honesty', also appears as 'integrity'.[35]

As we have seen, by contrast, western integrity endures an ever-growing split between entity and standards, between the two aspects of its dual meaning. It is a result of the intensifying flux of new and competing entities that are inherent in the western drive for expansion. An incidental result is that spirit has lost its hold on the imagination.[36]

The result of widespread secularization in the West, following on from that near monopoly and the subsequent loss of control over public life by organized religion, is that spirit can hardly be invoked in public speech.[37] When it is, usually it happens in an entirely mundane way, perhaps in connection with sport.[38] If the British talk of the 'Dunkirk spirit', the episode in the Second World War when their soldiers survived the Nazi onslaught and, taking to the boats, retreated across the Channel from France, then it is, more often than not, with tongue in cheek. Though it may be that Covid-19 has changed that a bit, prompting rather more serious calls on the 'national spirit'.

The affinity and reciprocal relationship between integrity and spirit indicates they both belong to a much wider creative process, the coming into being of new aspirations, objects and people. What philosophers have called ontology is as much about practice as existence, about how things are created as much as what is there to start with. And when their creator dies, the creations survive.

If the mundane repetitiousness of everyday life obscures the evidence of creation, it comes to our attention more often in the emergence of heroes. They make us face the possibility of radical novelty, and in their exceptional behaviour show us how individuals can make a difference. They offer a transcending novelty beyond ideology and religious boundaries, but whether they are saints or demons is never disclosed in advance.

It was the intuitive understanding of the interlocking of the physical and the cultural that explains the longevity of the idea of integrity. Its all-embracing quality has accompanied western history going back to Roman times, and it has expanded in scope to match the West's own experience. Indeed, in the West's expansion the clarification and extension of concepts has been part and parcel of its experience of a wider world.

Conceptualizing culture as a distinct sphere of meaning was equally a counterpart to and advanced by imperialism. It was intimately connected with the dynamics of western expansion. There is an example of this interconnection in his book on culture and imperialism by the great American literary scholar Edward W. Said. He pointed to the way Jane Austen's novel *Mansfield Park* (1814) made a mere handful of 'subliminal' references to the West Indian island of Antigua in a tale of a household and its linked families, their relationships and romances, on an English early nineteenth-century estate. In fact, the owner of the estate was absent for a long period attending to his plantation in Antigua, and Said remarked on the parallelism of his role in charge of both properties, although it was only for the English one that there was any extensive account.[39]

For both Austen and Said, one might equally remark there is a 'subliminal' reference to integrity. In her case, there were just three mentions in respect of her two main characters. In the case of the owner's son, Edmund Bertram, 'There was a charm, perhaps in his sincerity, his steadiness, his integrity' and 'the scruples of his integrity', in each mentioning his attraction to a woman.[40] Both references were to a potential marriage that would have prevented him or any man having 'fullest dependence on her faith and integrity' of the other main character, Fanny Price.[41] The only ones with integrity eventually found their true love in each other in the culmination of the novel. Rare references they may be, but strategic for focalizing the two key actors in the novel.

In Said's extensive comments, he only uses the word once, in a section headed 'The Cultural Integrity of Empire'.[42] So prominent and challenging a use demands explanation, and there is none. The section is part of a chapter with the title 'Consolidated Vision' and, overall, the impression is that imperialism is a mixture of cultures and identities and as such is an entity linked to many others. Said's last page includes, 'Survival in fact is about the connections between things.'[43] That existential comment may itself be sufficient to justify writing of the 'cultural integrity' of empire.

Throughout Said's exploration of the way cultures are, at one and the same time, hybrid and un-monolithic and yet distinct, he seeks to weave a way through the misunderstandings that arise in cultural contact and through the development of cultures over time. In his introduction to his book, he feels bound to reach out to less subtle advocates of national identity: 'Despite its extraordinary diversity, the United States is, and will surely remain, a coherent nation.'[44]

'Coherent'? A superb swerve through a linguistic minefield, or a weasel word? Certainly, an 'integrated nation' would have allowed too much scope for sociological debate, while a 'nation of integrity' would suffer the incredulity of realist political scientists. Does any nation have integrity?

Working for integrity

Examples of living memorials to the past are also evidence of the human desire to shape the future for coming generations. It is not just the continuity between past and future that is guaranteed, as in the Crystal Palace Park that commemorates the Great Exhibition of 1851. Closer to our own time, there is a vivid example in the World Trade Centre memorial to the 2,997 people who died when the twin towers were destroyed on the 11 September 2001.[45]

That desire extends into the daily activities and imaginations of countless people, directly and indirectly. The consequences reach indefinitely beyond the place and its visitors today or any day. In this sense, we can say those places have a 'spirit'. It is intimately related to maintaining its integrity, and that is a practical daily concern for all who care to be involved. In my own experience, this can become an explicit aspect of consultancy work. The following example involved analysis and advice to a local authority in Scotland. It took place at the very time the world was focused on honour and integrity in the White House, or its lack thereof.

The context was the crisis in a medium-sized Scottish industrial town, Falkirk, with a population of around 145,000, situated halfway between Glasgow and Edinburgh. It included Grangemouth, once the site of the largest oil refinery in Britain, owned by the oil giant BP, employing around 2,500 employees, which was considering closure of the oil-refining business.

BP's own concern led them to support a newly established consultancy and think tank, the International Futures Forum (IFF), based in Scotland, to partner Falkirk Council's own scoping of future risks and options. In April 2001, its founder, former diplomat Graham Leicester, organized an inaugural meeting at St Andrews, Scotland, where more than twenty-five professionals, intellectuals and activists met to explore a 'second Enlightenment'.[46] A small sub-group shared an interest in integrity. Anthony Hodgson had his own consultancy named 'Decision Integrity'.[47] We discussed the complexities of global/local linkages with Graham Leicester and Andrew Lyon from the Scottish Council Foundation

By the time of the second meeting of IFF in St Andrews in November 2001, several project papers on global and local integrity were being exchanged, and we advanced the idea that integrity should replace integration as a core concept and that we could think of social entities as 'integrities'.[48]

IFF was invited to the area in April 2002 for an extended deep dive to seek a more open and generous response. What became quickly apparent were the growing tensions between the Grangemouth community, BP and the town. Following this engagement, the director of Community Services (first Steve Dunlop and from 2003 Maureen Campbell) responded by producing a plan that came to be known as 'My Future's in Falkirk'. Afterwards, the rigidities of the relations of communities within Falkirk came to be replaced by a progressive provision for each according to their needs and, while it had originally felt left behind, over the next five years, not only Grangemouth, but all the sixteen constituent communities came to engage in a variety of different ways with the town of Falkirk as a whole. After INEOS bought the Grangemouth terminal in April 2005, the Council invited IFF to do a full repeat case study along the lines of the original one in 2002. What emerged was a story of determined response to the original crisis and moving beyond it to a new prospect for the future.

The Falkirk episode tells us a lot about integrity in illustrating fundamental processes in community formation. Before the crisis, Falkirk and within it Grangemouth were in uneasy coexistence, each holding on to what they had. The plan looked to integrate the people of Grangemouth into the town. The INEOS purchase and reorganization of the oil terminal provided the impetus both for movement out of Grangemouth and new opportunities within. It stimulated investment in a new business park nearby called the Falkirk Gateway.

A retired couple summed up the process when they told me Grangemouth held its identity through looking both outwards and inwards, and it looked to a consequent rejuvenation. The same applied to Falkirk as a whole: 'We will strive to become the focus of a new Scottish network of travel, tourism and employment opportunities' was one part of its vision statement.

In sum, the integrities of both Falkirk and its Grangemouth community were established through aspirations beyond their present state and in reaching out to the world beyond. Their identity was secured through engagement beyond themselves, not by retiring within it. This is inherent in anything to which integrity is attached. The standards to which it aspires carry its wholeness forward, while the end state remains always elusive.[49]

6

Being Human

Our story of the origin, rise and continuing transformation of the idea of integrity demands that we stand back and consider how such a construct, so specific to the West, compares with the broader context of ideas of what it is to be human in a world we have not made. There are deep assumptions around that theme that lie behind ways of life that distinguish civilizations from each other.

Do we live in a world of separate things? Or are we inextricably bonded into the seamless cloth of nature? Saying yes to one and no to the other sets us off on the course that has separated the West and the rest for two millennia. Can philosophical reasoning lead us in a new direction, perhaps beyond both?

The perennial dilemma

When philosophers examine ideas of reality and existence, they call it ontology. It has not been my purpose to contribute to philosophy, rather to the history of the present. But, as we have seen, the way integrity has been invoked in the past either challenges existence or is evidence of existential anxiety.

But our past engagement with integrity is a very special, unique historical course, differing in fundamental respects from the experience of the rest of the world. If we want to follow the idea of integrity through to its widest possible application, then, for the sake of everyone in the world, we need to bring the issues it raises into a frame that is beyond the West and the rest.

My chosen example for the contrast on fundamental existential issues will be Chinese civilization. In it, from time immemorial, *dao* is the way things bond in harmony with their environment and with nature in general, and that includes human beings. It is an outlook that stresses relations rather than autonomy and therefore has no concept equivalent to integrity.

The combination of wholeness and values in integrity means it should rate as a central concept in social theory. But over the centuries the atomism of western thought triumphed over the synoptic vision that would have helped that to happen. The philosophy of Epicurus in ancient Greece imagined a world of things. The Roman poet Lucretius rendered it thus: 'the nature of the universe, therefore, as it is in itself, is made up of two things; for there are bodies, and there is void.'[1]

In western thought, this emptiness that Lucretius found beyond each single thing prevailed through to the last century. It is not the only possible way to view existence. In the broadest perspective, the anthropologist Paul Radin argued for a 'consistent evolutionism and preoccupation with problems of origin among primitive peoples', and of their attempts 'to develop some systematized theory of the nature of things'.[2]

The Rumanian historian of religion Mircea Eliade pointed to the way 'cosmogonic' myths might be linked to the failure of crops: 'they expect the regeneration of cosmic life not from its restoration but from its recreation' (Fijians), or with healing the sick, 'the patient goes over the mythical history of the world' (Navajos).[3]

Yet, when that experience involves the cumulative record of a past, in other words when it has become history rather than myth, then recognition grows of the contribution of human beings to the creative process. But then, like the seasons, our achievements also pass away. Thus the ancient Romans were obsessed with the possibility of the end of all they had accomplished.[4]

It is when the mythology of a people is linked to territorial expansion that the sense of irreversibility and the genuine creative capacity of human beings begins to come into the foreground. 'For the Scandinavians . . . taking of a territory was equivalent to a repetition of Creation'[5] (which prompts the thought that perhaps the Vikings should be credited with the original drivers behind western expansionism.)

As far as the distinctiveness of the western experience is concerned, there is no way we can underestimate the impact on the worldview of the ancient Romans of the Christian belief in a God who created all things. Creativity was baked into the medieval Catholic worldview of the role of God.

The subsequent freedom from central Church control in the Reformation released new energies, even as integrity became a matter of individual conscience. It was God and their consciences that inspired the Pilgrim Fathers to cross the ocean to make a new life in an unknown territory. As we have seen, it was a challenge that required explicit commitments to integrity.

Integrity for modern western philosophers

If there were to be a science of the human condition, as opposed to a plethora of specialized disciplines, then integrity would have to be a central concept. Perhaps the nearest aspiration to provide such an all-encompassing view of our world came

from the post-Second World War writers known as existen-
tialists, like Jean-Paul Sartre, with his celebrated tome *Being
and Nothingness*.[6]

Actually, Sartre only mentions integrity at the very end of
his Conclusion where he reflects briefly on the possibility of
knowing a relationship. He asserts that because each one in
it denies he or she is the other person, then each is prevented
'from ever grasping it in its integrity'.[7] Similarly, his translator
Mary Warnock left it to the penultimate paragraph to write
that a hero 'is essentially *not* a political man; for he cares only
for his own integrity'.[8]

I find something telling in the way both Sartre and Warnock
allude to integrity only after examining the vast ramifications
of freedom in a world human beings have not made (in his
case, after 624 pages in the English translation). Their intricate
and often recondite arguments (like examining in depth the
precise meaning of the action of one person laying a hand
on another's) ultimately lead to them hanging from the single
thread of integrity.

While integrity figures so rarely in books of serious intellec-
tual depth, those instances when it does repay close attention.
We can turn to two that only consider integrity in passing
but which in their day achieved canonical status, John Rawls's
A Theory of Justice (1971) and Ronald Dworkin's *A Matter of
Principle* (1985).

Rawls's volume set the terms of academic debate on justice
for the next thirty years. On the face of it, integrity has a very
modest place indeed, mentioned twice in five hundred pages.
There he points to times when people lose faith in established
values and, in that context, he proceeds to say, 'there is a ten-
dency to fall back on the virtues of integrity: truthfulness and
sincerity, lucidity and commitment, or, as some would say,
authenticity.'[9]

That selection of five virtues that Rawls chooses to subsume
under integrity is interesting in its own right, and for what

it does not include. There is no place for instance in the list for autonomy, honour, independence or self-sufficiency. And overall, when put together, his list of virtues does not even guarantee a high moral quality for integrity. But then that suggests, rightly to my mind, that integrity is not itself one of the virtues, but rather a bearer or a container for them.

He adds a further important comment that tends to confirm that view and makes it clear he has adopted a highly nuanced position. He allows for integrity to be bad (recall my earlier account of Tom Driberg in chapter 4), suggesting a tyrant can also display the same virtues. The virtues themselves only become moral when 'joined to the appropriate conception of justice, one that allows for autonomy and objectivity correctly understood'. We can infer then that in the well-ordered society, where autonomy of the person and objectivity of judgement, intrinsic to justice, are guaranteed, integrity is safeguarded. In other words, for integrity to be moral it requires objective conditions to be fulfilled.

In that sequence of ideas, Rawls, by bringing autonomy and objectivity into the equation, is implicitly allowing for the more expansive dualism of integrity, at once moral and cognitive, to have a place as important as justice in understanding human society. Putting those additional qualities together with the virtues that belong to it generates the complex breadth of meaning of integrity in human affairs that we have encountered in this book.

Equally, it is a sequence of thought that links integrity with society, therefore emphasizing its centrality for understanding the human condition. We may have an inkling of Rawls's later appreciation of the significance of that point when, in the second and revised edition of his book, he includes the following in the last paragraph of a new preface: 'As a political conception, then, justice as fairness includes no natural right of private property in the means of production (although it does include a right to personal property as necessary for citizens' independence and integrity), nor a natural right to worker-owned and -managed firms.'[10] In that bland way, Rawls settles for liberal democracy as opposed to communism. And, we are bound to conclude, the integrity of the citizen is central to it. We may or may not agree with the conclusion, but the argument lodges integrity in it as a central premise.

Similarly to Rawls, Ronald Dworkin's massive and rightly celebrated volume defined a major field of philosophical argument in the latter part of the last century. Also similarly, it seems to allow integrity to creep in by the side gate. Yet again, it raises questions about the basis of society, for he links it to civil disobedience and questions of conscience.

Dworkin cites the possible reaction of a person in the United States, living at a time when a Fugitive Slave Act was in force, who was confronted with a fleeing slave at his door. The act required him to turn the slave over to the authorities. 'His personal integrity, his conscience, forbids him to obey.'[11] In what Dworkin calls this '"integrity-based" civil disobedience', the homeowner was in the same situation as soldiers drafted into a war they deemed wicked. (In 2023, we may have a heightened appreciation of the long-term significance of this lightly veiled reference to the American Civil War.) We should note his equation of integrity with conscience. Like integrity, conscience is not in itself a virtue, simply the place for virtues to be heard.

There were two other kinds of civil disobedience. One was where Blacks broke the law in segregated communities by sitting at forbidden lunch counters. They were simply claiming rights, as were the protestors against the Vietnam War (though here they were claiming the rights of others). This was for Dworkin '"justice-based" civil disobedience'. (There was also a third type of policy-based civil disobedience where the objective is simply to change dangerously unwise policies.) He distinguished between the first two types of disobedience by pointing to the purely defensive and conscience-based nature of the former, as opposed to the instrumental nature of the latter, an attempt to get a political programme changed. It is here that we are obliged to recognize the crossover in the ways Rawls and Dworkin bring the discussion of integrity and justice together.

They point to the inescapable conclusion that the integrity of the individual and the integrity of society are not necessarily compatible with each other. But in this respect, it is consistent with our account of the inner tensions that powered the crossings to America and the creation of new communities.

What I called in chapter 3 the pulse of modernity powered the West's expansion for half a millennium. For a clearer view of how specific this is to the West, we should travel as far as possible to the East where quite different views of the human condition have been lodged in everyday outlooks from the earliest recorded time.

Alternative wisdom from the East

In Chinese culture we can find an idea that has occupied a similar pivotal position to integrity in the West but for much longer. From the earliest times, *dao* has been recognized as the governing concept for all existence and thought. Lao Zi, born in the sixth century before Christ, described it thus: 'The *dao* gives birth to the unified thing (one), the one splits itself into two opposite aspects, the two gives birth to another (three), the newborn three produces myriad things. The myriad things have *yin* and *yang* within themselves as opposing forces. *Yin* and *yang* interact and are unified into harmony in *qi*, the vital energy.'[12]

This is a synoptic view of all reality as an unbroken and limitless extension of connections between things. Lao Zi's sayings about *dao* emphasize it as beyond description, as the originating, governing force for all things. *Dao* belongs to nature and to human beings; it takes things forward and then back again; heaven follows *dao*, and everything under heaven finds fulfilment in *dao*; the wise have *dao* and their advice to a ruler rejects force.

Dao has regularly been translated into English as 'the way'. This conveys an affinity with the Christian ideas of following the way and the life of Christ. But it is a stretch too far to make it a theological notion. The English word 'nature' is much closer to the pervasive and comprehensive scope of *dao*. In English, there is talk of the nature of things. There is human nature, nature in general and in particular. What is natural and what is unnatural both belong to people and to the world outside them. They can follow nature and they belong to 'Nature', often capitalized, the physical environment around that they have not created.

There the parallel between nature and *dao* stops. Unlike *dao*, nature has no answer to how things began. It has no creation myth. It begs for the answers to how a world of things began, the big question that prompted Lucretius to compose his epic *On the Nature of Things*.

We have arrived at a profound difference between the axioms of the Chinese worldview and the atomistic vision that the West singled out of the much more diverse speculations of the ancient world. The image of a world of things was elaborated into a story where all beings were created by a single God, an all-powerful Creator who made the Earth and all that was in it, human beings, too. *Dao* provides a story of the origin of all things and their subsequent interrelation, but there is no Creator, no agent that could one day be emulated by those He had created.

Christianity's rise provided comfort for people living in a world of disconnected things. It provided solace in the confusion of the declining Roman Empire. The wisdom of the creator God commanded the principles underlying the natural world and provided the morality that people could not find in their own too human nature. Those principles, both natural and moral, were also accessible to the reason that the Almighty had given to human beings. The creator God had made a world of things that could be explored. He motivated a quest for knowledge, of the natural and human world. He inspired science; he travelled with voyages of discovery.

The journey that the idea of integrity has followed parallels the story of the expansion of the western world. It is the idea of an object that holds together by virtue of principles that come from outside it. By contrast, the world of *dao* is one where the bonds between people and people, between them and everything else, exist in harmony under heaven. People follow *dao* and realize their place in the world. They live in the middle realm (*zhonguo*, the name for China), the stable point in that space under heaven.

Integrity in the West is a precarious achievement. The gap between standards that society proclaims and the necessities of everyday living is repeatedly too wide to be bridged. Integrity is a state of being that is always under threat, being constructed and reconstructed. When the world outside is in flux, the search for integrity can become a painful preoccupation, a source of despair rather than hope. No wonder some prefer to ignore it altogether!

Chinese, therefore, like any non-Latinate language, has problems in translating integrity. While the meaning of completeness or wholeness can be translated '完整' [wan zheng] (wholeness), the moral aspects appear as '正直' [zhengzhi] (uprightness) and '诚实' [cheng shi] (honesty), and at other times are translated as '诚信' [cheng xin] (good faith), or '操守' [cao shou] (moral principle).[13]

These various terms used in the translation of integrity do not prevent us looking for one where they are most closely related to each other. Arguably, in Chinese, that is represented by the idea of the complete or consummate man (完人) [wan ren]. In this respect we have the reported sayings of Confucius to help us. When his student Tzu-lu asked him what a complete man was, he said: 'A man as wise as Tsang Wu-chung [politician], as free from desires as Meng Kung-chuo [high-ranking official], as courageous as Chuang-tzu of Pien [soldier] and as accomplished and versatile as Jan Ch'iu [Confucius' student] who is further refined by the rites and music, may be considered a complete man.' Then he added: 'But to be a complete man nowadays one need not be all those things.' Staying honest, willing to risk his life in a good cause and holding to lifelong standards in all circumstances are sufficient.[14]

The modern Chinese philosopher Feng Youlan (1895–1990) went further to explain what a complete man means. He lives in *tian* [天] (the sky) and *di* [地] (the earth) realm. He consciously regards himself not only as a member of his society, but also as a member of the *yuzhou* [宇宙] (cosmos). He knows about *dao* and understands the limits of worldly affairs, so that his virtue is realized in the goal of melting in and combining with the virtue of nature.[15]

None of this is remote from an account of a Christian person of integrity, with one profound difference. The integrity of the Christian does not melt into and combine with the virtue of nature.

The Janus-faced concept

'Entity' is a word we have used for things. As a term for human creations, it has the advantage of suggesting some kind of completeness. It can therefore figure in judgements of integrity. Persons, countries, homes, offices and temples are all entities, and in each case we can, and do, judge their integrity.

It is the vast scope of integrity, the sheer extent of its actual and possible applications, which explains why it has to be placed within the widest possible context. Integrity, for human beings, relates to standards and values, but its scope extends beyond human beings to the products of their creative activity, as we saw in chapter 5, and beyond them to all other things in the world.

Can we then say integrity is not a value at all? We can list values like courage, humility, cooperation, justice, beauty and truth, and then see integrity as distinct from them. It can cast its capacious blanket over them all and require them to coexist in a single entity. Its scope is all that holds the entity together. Alasdair MacIntyre concludes a discussion of the nature of the virtues by writing that there is at least one virtue, integrity (he adds constancy, too) that cannot be specified without referring to the 'wholeness of human life'.[16] If it is a virtue, then it has a very special status.

The two meanings of integrity, adherence to high standards or striving for values on the one hand, being whole or complete on the other, are puzzling when they can so obviously be at odds with each other. When we consider integrity as it applies to persons and try to treat each meaning independently, we can see how quickly the paradoxes mount.

Can we think of persons having integrity when they are expressing themselves fully and presenting a clear and unambiguous image to the world, even as, at the same time, they advocate and practice violence against ethnic minorities? In other words, can a racist have integrity? Is there such a thing as bad integrity?

Conversely, what are we to think of the highly respected person, known for uprightness and strict observance of a moral code, who can't begin to perform at work because of the effort needed to dispel forbidden thoughts? Can you have sick or fragmented integrity?

Integrity has the face of the classical god Janus. It looks both ways, reaches deep into the person or the social entity, holding personality or mission, subconscious desires and basic needs together (authenticity) but also stretches outwards to the values, ideas and fundamental tenets (principles) that swirl around in that primal soup we call culture.

Is integrity more a matter of conformity to principles, or rather is it to be equated with the wholeness of an entity? It has to be both, and as such exists in a sphere which is neither purely culture nor entirely in the material world, but a composite of them. The entities that have integrity are, in a very precise and literal sense, cultural beings. (Recall that cultural beings also include human collectivities, as well as the products of human design.)

Cultural beings (or entities) in general have this double-sided nature. The qualities attributed to persons depend on both performance and recognition. Modesty, respect, care and humility are all culturally defined, communicated through others and personally delivered. Think of celebrity, an extreme example, and how both personal behaviour and media communication are essential for its manufacture.[17]

If we understand that the wholeness of principled behaviour has a base in culture, we then also take on board the fact that it will vary from culture to culture. It follows from our account that this will happen in two main ways. First, the principles that contribute to the wholeness may vary in time and place, but secondly it will not be the person that is the primary site of integrity – it may be the family, kinship group, tribe, sect or community.

In the West, the separation of the individual from all those local social anchorages has become so pronounced that even human society as such is thought of as the ultimate source of values. At the same time, a culture that values individualism makes integrity a high and demanding expectation, projecting the person onto a high and lonely pedestal. We shall see how shaky that position has become.

The integrity crisis that prompted this book was one where the din around integrity drowned out the globalization message of the Clinton presidency.[18] But at the time of writing we are still in the ongoing crisis that began with the end of the Trump presidency and the storming of the Capitol Building on 6 January 2021. On this occasion, the very institutions of American democracy were in extreme danger.

A central argument of this book has been that integrity becomes the key word of the moment, a cry for help when nothing seems to be safe. Our story has been very much one of the interplay between two subjects: a changing world, flux, currently globalization, on the one hand, and the loss and struggle to maintain integrity on the other.

Integrity as an idea is everywhere, at least in the claim to it, and in the accusation of its absence. We can see it in the law, in people, in buildings, in nature, in our imaginations, sometimes in our faces, more often in the background. Just because of its pervasive presence, do we need to treat it as a top priority? Do we have to give it greater importance in our decisions than anything else?

If integrity pops up in so many contexts, without further explanation, it may be because it does appear to have an imme-diate intelligibility that requires no further comment. A bit like the air we breathe – though in these days of the integrity vacuum, that can't be taken for granted as it might have been once.

Alternatively, integrity may be a shibboleth, with no real meaning save to adorn the banner of those who rise to the top. Indeed, it may fit well with postmodern accounts of our time, be just a floating signifier attached to anything or everything without any real meaning. But when its past has been so deeply embedded in dominant western outlooks, the idea that it no longer has relevance for the present-day world cries out for deeper examination.

The incomplete journey

In the past, there have been two major advances in western thought that come closer to the problem of giving full weight to the links between wholeness and values. The first was the development of systems thinking. Originally an old idea, going back to Isaac Newton and earlier, it recognizes that the interconnection of its parts is crucial to the survival of an entity, and that those links are governed by principles, in this case laws of nature.[19]

The second was the effort to identify the special features of social entities, especially societies, and to propose integration as the overall process, with shared values at the centre. This was the major sociological project we saw associated with Talcott Parsons in the mid-twentieth century. Marxist critics pointed to the inevitable solipsism of this account since the systemic features of a society pointed to its bonds with the world around it.[20]

It has frequently teased the western mind to figure out how Marxism has been officially grafted onto traditions of Chinese thought going back to Confucius and earlier. The secret is that in both cases social relations take on central importance. There is then no sense in China that the adoption of Marxism today means a rupture with ancient Chinese thought. It merely amounts to a modern elaboration of age-old understanding to account for the condition of society in contemporary industrialism.

It is also the case that Marx's upbringing in an educated cosmopolitan German-Jewish family gave him the basis for an independent outlook on the motivations of Christian-based capitalism. He was prepared to be the marginal intellectual critic of the society he saw around him, and of the self-proclaimed universalism of Hegelian philosophy. Thus, for China too, Marx provides an entry into the western past as well as into the contradictions of capitalism by a critic who had first-hand experience of it.

For the greatest contrast, Chinese philosophy originated in a quite different understanding of the place of human beings in the world. We have seen how it contrasts fundamentally with the atomism, creationism and individualism associated with the rise of integrity in western thought. Convergence in our time with these alternative assumptions can be found in many trends in western thought. There is a new emphasis on interdependence with nature for instance, and in the idea of ecological civilization.

In these respects, we can view human advance as one where West and East join in combatting the threats to human life on this planet. If this sharing means the relative decline of the West, then it will be to the advantage of our species as a whole. One example of creative sharing is in the intersection of biology, systems theory and evolution.

There are grounds for hope. In recent years in the West, the ecological movement has stressed the intimate and mutual interdependencies between human beings and nature. Its inspirational moment came with James Lovelock's Gaia hypothesis of the interdependence of organisms and environments.[21]

Effectively this brings the western idea of civilization together with the Daoist notion of the continuous pulse of existence. The civilizations of East and West come together as one. In that context, integrity will be absorbed into the ongoing human task of creating itself and its own future on and beyond this planet. If that journey's goal is ultimate objectivity, its complement is ultimate subjectivity.

In essence, these ideas have brought human history and evolution together and underlie the idea of ecological civilization as a prerequisite for the survival of both the species and the planet. It became a stated goal of the Chinese Communist Party in 2007 and has since been adopted within the discourse of the United Nations. The International Forum on Ecological Civilization has held annual conferences since 2009.

We need to find the requirements to be recognized as parties to the course of history. We have to face up to all those features of human agency that mean we can identify its course with our own purposes: identity, respect, recognition and responsibility. Above all, we need to recognize creativity as the bridge that we make with, and a driver for, evolution.

To my mind, the thinker in the last century who came closest to escaping the dead ends that have afflicted western ideas of integrity was Hannah Arendt. Like Marx, she came from a quite different personal and intellectual background from the dominant western intellectuals. By contrast with their disciplined, secular, almost ascetic style of argument, her intimate engagement with ancient Greek thought prompted her to break away from a conventional account of the problems of her own time.

Arendt's insistence on the importance of human beings in the plural was consistent with Karl Marx's placing of social relations at the centre of his concerns.[22] Both were Jewish, halfway between West and East one might say. Indeed, it is even further to the East that we had to go to find relations, rather than things or individuals, both entities, as the starting point for understanding our world.

In *The Human Condition*, first published in 1958, Arendt declared the launch of the space satellite to be more important than the splitting of the atom. The prospect of leaving the Earth impressed her more than the threat to human existence. It matched her assertion that the promise of natality, not inevitable mortality, was the miracle that saves the world.

It may have been this optimism, extraordinary in view of what she had lived through, which saved her from the dour outlook on integrity that afflicts anyone who finds its elusiveness daunting. She considers personal integrity in conjunction with individual sovereignty and rejects the common assumption that together they mean freedom. She calls that a 'basic error'.

For her, the idea of winning untouchable integrity and therefore freedom implies domination of everyone else. It is a failure to recognize that 'No man can be sovereign because not one man, but men inhabit the earth.'[23] For her, action itself depends on the plurality of human beings. She goes on to write that the moral code is 'entirely based on the presence of others'.[24]

From the plurality of others, it is only a short step to the multiplicity of relationships. In her terms, it is the human capacity for freedom that produces 'the web of human relationships'.[25] This web arises out of the acting and speaking of people to each other. It is in between, intangible, but no less real than tangible objects.[26]

For Arendt, this is the realm of human affairs, existing wherever people live together. It took her into the deeper meaning of the circumnavigation of the globe or the mastery of flight. She recognized it was the process of communication with others that created a world. The advance of communication technology in the digital age has only added emphasis to an insight that remains as valid today as it did a century ago.

For reassurance that integrity has continuing relevance, especially when its loss is trumpeted so widely, we need close analysis that places it in the centre field of concepts that have occupied the attention of the West's most prominent thinkers. It requires a place alongside reason, responsibility, trust, community, justice and democracy. Establishing that status is still work in progress.

A significant contributor to that work is the distinguished American public intellectual and legal scholar, Stephen L. Carter. His analysis of the concept is the most profound we have to date, where we have a wide-ranging consideration of integrity's relation to American core values, together with an exploration of the dilemmas it raises in practice. It is a nuanced account, as his discussion of the abortion issue indicates: 'it is possible to say, with no sense of irony, that both sides are right.'[27]

The culmination of Carter's book is an extended consideration of the key issue of whether there can be evil integrity. His answer basically is that it is impossible since integrity depends on the ability to discern what is good and bad. That may appear to allow too much room for radical relativism, but on the account here we can add that following a principle is inherent in what is good, and opportunism negates that. Lack of principles opens the way to evil results. Ultimately, it leads to what remains to this day the greatest evil, genocide. When Carter was writing in the 1990s, he saw it exemplified in Bosnia. But he still trembled for his country when thinking of Vietnam.[28]

The very all-embracing potential relevance of integrity means it may also exhaust its ability to provide closure. Indeed, the quest for integrity chases ever receding goals. There can be no end to a search for equality, or for self-realization, or for justice, and yet for each a check for integrity along the way provides a reflexive assessment of travel towards a destination along a long and winding road. But it is a pilgrim's progress in a secular world.

Integrity is about existence and what as human beings we contribute to it. Those who have inherited the West's concepts and products are free to use it in the ways they find illuminating, creative or challenging. Whether filled with karma or with *dao* or another cosmic intuition, it is inherently always open to exploration, change and renewal. May it be at least one western contribution to the human future that invites sharing and does not bring suffering with it.

7

Media Storms in the New Century

If the language of spirit has largely dropped out of western public life, it is because it is mainly suffused with images and discourse that inhabit media space. The spirit of the age was a concept familiar to the eighteenth and nineteenth centuries but lapsed in the twentieth. Now, it lurks anonymously in the media of communication, print, visual and social.[1] In that spirit, integrity occupies a central and contested place.

In 1997, President Bill Clinton consolidated his second term of office by taking the idea of globalization out of the business schools and Wall Street and turning it into a mission for all America.[2] But for the whole of the very next year, through to February 1999, he had to defend himself against allegations of sexual relations with a White House intern. The point-counterpoint of integrity versus globalization was then played out in a protracted contest for the next presidency of the United States.

It happened again – a media storm about the integrity of national leaders. This time integrity became headline material in the United States and the United Kingdom throughout 2022. From the gravity of the assault on the Capitol in Washington in early January to the revelations of drinking parties after work during the Covid lockdowns in London's Number 10, ultimately it was the integrity of western statesmen that was repeatedly brought into question.

Each time integrity was raised, the world was inscribed in the character faults of its leaders. But these are not unique events. Media storms over integrity were a repeated feature of American public life before and during the Bush Jr presidency. They occur again in the so-called integrity vacuum of the last few years.

Everything points to an epochal shift in this century as profound as the one we described when Machiavelli gave advice to the Italian ruler of the time in *The Prince*. The pretence to have integrity was part and parcel of what came to be known as the political realism of the new modern age. That was a blatant disregard for the established Church and for the advice of its clerical intellectuals throughout the medieval period. But, for the public view, all was religious observance, piety and devotion.

But today a new disdain for integrity has replaced even pretence. The celebrity politician makes his (normally male) mark in media presenting game shows and competitions. There his person will be exposed to the scrutiny of viewers and the avalanche of social media posts that follows, the more the better. Short of complicity in murder, everything contributes to fame and political fortune. It marks the fantasy politics of the digital age, a shift as profound as that which took place in the sixteenth century.

Restoring 'Honor and Integrity': Bush vs Clinton

For Bill Clinton, in upbeat mood, the celebration of the upcoming millennium set the seal on his presidency, but even more on the American century. In the 1990s, the United States basked in the collapse of the Soviet Union and the end of the Cold War. American capitalism was triumphant.

Back on the last day of 1999, in his speech ushering in the new century, he had defined what for him was most important to the nation in the coming century: 'It will require us to share with our fellow Americans, and increasingly with our fellow citizens of the world, the economic benefits of globalization, the political benefits of democracy and human rights.'[3] As a rider, he added, 'We may not be able to eliminate all the harsh consequences of globalization', but he hoped trade could work in a way that would benefit ordinary working families. Always the master communicator, both listening as well as speaking, he was well attuned to the rising discontent among those deaf to, and left behind by, his signature tune, globalization. Only a month earlier, the size of anti-globalization protests in Seattle had forced him to pull out of a World Trade Organization meeting.

No one could better his rhetorical skills. He could acknowledge the aspects of globalization that might represent a threat to many ordinary Americans, jobs displaced by imports and communities contending with foreign immigration. He offered soothing words rather than solutions, but words were not enough. Globalization was so much an anthem for his presidency that he could not drop it, especially when he had to bridge the major hiatus in his term of office. Considered from a world standpoint, where men of power in any civilization have always taken advantage of young women, the publicity surrounding an ephemeral private episode is unusual.

Special then, but more to the point, the concern for integrity belongs to the unique story of the West from its very beginnings. Indeed, we have already seen in Shakespeare that integrity is at the heart of an archetypal myth: female virtue as the foundation of world order.

The assaults on Clinton's character culminated in his impeachment by the House of Representatives, only for the Senate subsequently to reject the charges against him. But the protracted focus on his moral standards was to do lasting damage to the Democrats.[4]

When his vice-president Al Gore bid to be the next president, his chosen pitch of climate change only seemed even further away from those daily concerns. Voters worried more about local issues and moral standards. Moreover, for Republicans there were long-standing personal reasons to attack him. Gore had criticized George H. W. Bush Sr in his years as president (1989–93) for failing to act on global warming and had made himself the standard bearer for environmentalism in his book *Earth in the Balance* (1992).[5]

Integrity as a theme already had traction in public life well before George W. Bush adopted it. Indeed, it was his father, George H. W. Bush, who had established by Executive Order 12805, 11 May 1992, the Council on Integrity and Efficiency to conduct interagency and inter-entity audit and inspection throughout government. It was to be he who appointed the Inspectors General who made up the Council.

Integrity, Bush Sr long believed, could be an effective catch-all for his positions on abortion, balanced budget, religious freedom and the Equal Rights amendment. While he was vice-president, they had been summed up in a book of interviews on his career published as *George Bush: Man of Integrity* (1988), detailing his relationships with southern evangelists and serving as an effective background for a successful run for the presidency later in the year.

'Integrity and honour' became the watchwords for the Republican Party because in their view Clinton was vulnerable to attack on those qualities. That was even before the scandal of his relations with Monica Lewinsky captured the headlines. Having integrity was not in itself news or remarkable. It was a standard expectation for any respectable citizen. But its loss was.[6] For the American right, this was an additional source of strength for a campaign of national restoration, especially poignant for the son to revenge the defeat of his father after his one-term presidency. The family dynasty thus rose up to avenge the dishonour heaped on the nation by a disgraced president.

The presidential election of 2000 is remembered now for the contested election result, the so-called hanging chads of the disputed Florida contest, which could only be settled in the Supreme Court. It decided in favour of George W. Bush, the son of the 41st president of the United States. It was Clinton who had defeated George H. W. Bush in 1992. George W. therefore became the 43rd president, having campaigned on the slogan of restoring honour and integrity to the Oval Office.

These archetypical mythical themes – a past golden age, a fallen hero, a villainous destroyer of virtue, the son restoring greatness – could reach into the hidden depths of the collective imagination and help to explain how the claim to integrity can be immune to discordant facts. The tenacity of the Bush family's hold on that claim was such that it could secure George W.'s re-election in 2004.

That the Bush family had built its huge wealth on oil, munitions and arms did not amount to a stain on its record for a country that prided itself on military strength. Yet one might have thought that the financial support the family firm gave to the German war effort in the early 1940s, until the American government put a stop to it, ought to have been eye-popping enough.[7] But this was a buried distant past, and it wasn't sex. More extraordinary was the ease with which George W. was able to shrug off his close association with Kenneth Lay. He had been chief executive of Enron, the energy company that turned financial fiction into real life on a scale that made it the biggest corporate collapse in history.

In the past, Lay had given financial and practical support to George W. H. Bush. The company and its placemen were intimately involved in the first Bush administration. For George W., he became part of his team preparing for the presidential elections at the end of 2000.[8] On 1 December 2001,

Enron filed for bankruptcy. The administration dismissed it as a 'business scandal, not a political scandal'.[9]

President George W. Bush was thus able to sustain his claim to integrity in the face of prolonged attacks on his character over many years. It covered, of course, not just his famed 'misstatements', but also youthful misdemeanours and business dealings. The ease with which he was able to do this said more about the political system than it did about his abilities.

Everyone knew to what George W. Bush was alluding with 'honour and integrity'. It evoked the image of the stain on the dress of Clinton's intern, the young woman who had pleasured him in his working hours as president, the cause of his impeachment by Congress. It had left an even greater stain on his personal reputation for the mass of American voters.

No amount of stress on global challenges could compensate for moral failure. Thereafter, integrity became the Republican Party's repeated and most effective rhetorical weapon. An embittered Al Gore showed once more how he lacked Clinton's political skills by falling into the trap of using it to attack Bush.[10]

Gore announced in August 2003 that he would not run again for the presidency. He turned on Bush once again with the accusation of lacking 'honesty and integrity' in the period which led up to the Iraq War. He pointed to a failure to find nuclear weapons when Bush had warned of their presence, suggesting that access to oil was the main motivation for invasion.[11]

Bush had spoken of honour and integrity, Gore emphasized honesty and integrity: the difference between the two formulations matters. Honour includes pride, reputation, steadfastness, courage, respect, especially towards women; honesty requires telling the truth, refusing to conceal, refraining from theft. In terms of everyday life, arguably honesty has much more palpable consequences.

Campaigns against corruption are a political expression of its widespread recognition as a necessity for business and administration as well as in personal relations. They are commonplace beyond the West and need no boost from an idea of integrity. For Gore, lack of honesty meant Bush was unfit for the highest office. But he had bracketed it with integrity. In that respect, the completeness of the person also came into play, and in the United States enough of the electorate had given George W. Bush and 'honour and integrity' their votes, and twice over.

Media integrity storms 2004–8

In these early years of the twenty-first century, integrity became the ultimate reference for standards by which to judge anything that was controversial in public life. The rhetoric of integrity carried George W. Bush through his first term of office and into a second term, despite waging yet another of America's masochistic wars, this time in Iraq. That had previously looked like an opportunity for Democrat hopefuls in the run-up to the 2004 presidential election campaign.

Howard Dean, an early front runner for the Democrats in the Presidential campaign, was forthright in his opinion: 'President Bush came into office promising to bring honor and integrity to the White House. No more promises. It's time for accountability.'[12] Dean was widely applauded for his plain speaking, plain enough to be called 'venomous' by conservative columnist David Brooks.[13]

In the event, Dean made the old mistake of adopting the terms of debate of his likely opponent. Despite trying to highlight intelligence failures over Saddam Hussein's weaponry prior to the invasion of Iraq, he hadn't been able to resist raising integrity. Clearly, Bush had already marked up a significant success. It was *on his terms* that his opponents were debating with each other. They had effectively conceded to the

Republicans the all-important agenda-setting function for the early campaigns.

The integrity of the Democratic candidates for nomination remained a live issue into the New Year of 2004. Two of the most prominent commentators in American public life weighed in on the topic, David Brooks and Paul Krugman, in the pages of the *New York Times*.

Brooks, reviewing the candidates, treated 'integrity/ leadership' as one of three main categories on which to judge them. The other headings were simply 'domestic policy' and 'foreign affairs', terms without any implicit judgemental standards, referring only to fields of government. But 'integrity/ leadership' referred to the qualities of the person. Of the six runners, Brooks explicitly rated only Dick Gephardt as 'a man of integrity, who, putting his career at risk, has stuck tenaciously to his positions on war, trade and the working class.' This elaboration on the idea of integrity emphasized courage and consistency, reinforced by 'Also he is an experienced and fair-minded legislator'.[14]

One of the other runners that Brooks rated badly was General Wesley Clark: 'Two years ago, he lauded Bush and his "great team". Now he savages them with loopy conspiracy theories. Who is this guy and why aren't more of his military colleagues more enthusiastic supporters?'

'Who is this guy?' is rhetorical overkill, for, as we have seen, Clark had been in the headlines for months. But the implication is that Clark is an unknown quantity, a mystery being. In other words, his integrity is in question.

Four months after the CBS opinion poll, the heavyweight columnist and economics Nobel Prizewinner Paul Krugman weighed in. He sought to combine three separate accusations into one overall judgement on the lack of integrity in the Bush administration. Recalling 'honour and integrity', Krugman asked for these apologies: on the leak of the CIA agent's name; on obstruction of an inquiry into the 9/11 destruction of the

World Trade Center; on appointing a partisan to take charge of the Pentagon's Inspector General's office. Krugman concluded that Bush was getting away with things that no previous president could have done, and he asked: 'What's gone wrong with our country?'[15] His answer came with the outcome of the eventual presidential election. It suggested that anyone who unfurled the banner of integrity could overcome any misdeeds.

This was how George W. Bush celebrated his victory in the prepared text for his second inaugural address on 20 January 2005:

> In America's ideal of freedom, the public interest depends on private character – on integrity, and tolerance toward others, and the rule of conscience in our own lives. Self-government relies, in the end, on the governing of the self. . . . Americans move forward in every generation by reaffirming all that is good and true that came before – ideals of justice and conduct that are the same yesterday, today and forever.[16]

'Private character', 'Governing of the self' – pure effrontery from a man whose wayward youth had come near to undermining his original campaign for office. But, following Machiavelli, it was the outward show of integrity that mattered the most.

The presidential campaigns of 2008 provided an even more pronounced example of untouchability in Sarah Palin, former Alaska governor, darling of the American right and running mate for John McCain in his contest with Barack Obama. She had made a name for herself as a plain-speaking defender of traditional family values and exemplar of the common sense of the housewife. Palin evoked memories of Margaret Thatcher, but in a specifically American way, presenting her family as part of her political image, not simply something managed in the background. But then, plumb in the middle of her vice-presidential bid came the news that Palin's unmarried daughter was expecting a baby. Was the unplanned pregnancy a catastrophe? No, the conservative campaign treated it as a gift from God.

It led journalist Leon Wieseltier to reflect on the nature of integrity in an article for the magazine *New Republic*.[17] Palin, he declared, was a woman of integrity, and he didn't say this in a sardonic sense. He found nothing phoney about her: 'She is too immediately what she is. Palin is the sort of supporter of war in Iraq whose son is shipping off to the war in Iraq . . . Whatever the Christian conservative way of life is, Palin is living it.' This character assessment of Palin and of what he called a 'grotesque and fascinating candidacy' led Wieseltier further to raise what appears as one of the paradoxes of integrity, namely its 'moral insufficiency'. Stressing wholeness, he wrote: 'it is neutral about questions of truth and falsity, good and evil . . . A unified identity is not for that reason an admirable identity.'[18]

Having followed the story of the rhetoric of integrity up to now, we will notice that Wieseltier is offering a striking reversal of Machiavelli's doctrine. Pretence falls away. Unity of character is everything, warts and all. This takes us considerably further into the peculiarity of the western idea of integrity. It is so often simply paired with just one of honour, honesty, accountability or another of a myriad of values. But the pairing suggests it is more than these. It is distinct and separable, existing on a different plane. But is it beyond good and evil?

The big issues that arise here have claimed our attention throughout this book. Integrity seems on the one hand to have something like a superior quality. On the other hand, it appears to have no necessary and particular moral content. In other words, a moral person can do without it!

Beyond that, when the wholeness of the person is emphasized, it can extend to neutralizing moral content altogether. In this respect, the individual starts to resemble an impersonal object, larger than life or not even living at all, or inhabiting another plane of existence. Given the frequent occurrence of references to integrity in public life, and its use as the knockout blow in political debate, we are led to appreciate how its paradoxical qualities correspond to the moral ambiguities of political power, so clearly recognized by Machiavelli in the West or the Legalists in ancient China in their advice to rulers.

Integrity may appear as a mere rhetorical artifice, but on closer inspection it leads us to underlying realities of the human condition where power and values vie for our attention and rarely seem to be aligned with each other. Conflict and options define the field where claims to integrity arise.

But the frantic rush of accusations of lost integrity suggests a yearning for a time when all was reliable and moral. Despondency spreads from the sense of lost integrity. In its decline from that golden age, the present time feels discordant, chaotic and confusing. Politicians who claim to restore that bygone integrity raise expectations that lead to despair when the lost paradise fails to materialize.

The British integrity vacuum

'In the age of Putin's aggression, we should salute Gorbachev's integrity, says Boris', a newspaper headline that provides an appropriate bookend for the two crises that have shaped this book.[19] Gorbachev's death in August 2022 prompted a babel of tributes from world leaders, Biden and Putin included.

The irony of British Prime Minister Boris Johnson applauding Gorbachev's integrity could not have been lost on the home readership. He was about to be ejected from his head of government position after a series of missteps that made his integrity the calling card for every doorstep opinion pollster.

Johnson's own three-year record in the top job meant that integrity never left the headlines. As a former journalist himself, attuned to public discourse, he never shirked employing the term either. Integrity appeared in government legislation.

There was a plan for an 'electoral integrity bill' that would require every voter to prove identity with a photo ID.

The leftist liberal newspaper the *Guardian* declared in an editorial, '[T]his is a device for voter suppression that will damage the integrity of British democracy.'[20] The bill, nonetheless, became an Act of Parliament in April 2022. Indeed, independent research had shown that near to 100 per cent of the electorate already owned such an ID. 'Integrity of British democracy' was a high card to play when the stakes were so low.

In the downward spiral of events that led up to Johnson's resignation from Conservative Party leadership, and his eventual departure from the office of prime minister, integrity was repeatedly referred to as the missing element in his behaviour. While this book has sought to explore integrity in the broadest possible context, one has to grant that the Boris Johnson story provides a marvellous local British case study. His life and career offer the simple time frame of a personal biography, not the millennia we have covered previously. Much can be made of Johnson's privileged background. Eton College and Oxford University are enough to tick that box. But those august institutions can cover a multitude of sins – literally – as well as a lot of unhappiness.

Boris was moved from house to house thirty-two times before he was fifteen. By comparison, Eton must have been an oasis of stability, even if he plainly had brushes with authority. The *Times* journalist Rachel Sylvester quotes from one of his schoolteachers' reports: 'I think he honestly believes that it is churlish of us not to regard him as an exception, one who should be free of the network of obligation which binds everyone else.'[21] Sylvester also quotes Johnson, when he was mayor of London, telling one of his advisers, 'I'm never going to change. I am who I am.'[22]. In other words, his career challenges the idea that integrity combines wholeness with acceptance of society's rules. Here is another example of the paradox that attended Palin's reputation. Had Boris wished to prolong his career as prime minister, he might have chosen to observe the maxim that Machiavelli made notorious, namely, to maintain the appearance of integrity but not to have it.

Integrity, or more often the lack of it, had been a recurrent theme in British public discourse too. Back in March 2003, the BBC featured a claim that the British government had 'sexed up' (notice the terminology) its dossier on Iraq weapons to support going to war alongside the United States. Later disclosures revealed that prime minister Tony Blair and his officials saw it as an attack both on their integrity and 'the integrity of the process of government'.[23]

Integrity is big enough to feature on the front page of national newspapers. On 25 May 2020, the London-based *Daily Telegraph* ran this banner headline: 'Responsibly, legally and with integrity'. These were actually the words used the day before by Prime Minister Johnson when called upon to defend the behaviour of his top adviser, Dominic Cummings. Cummings had been caught by an onlooker breaking the Covid-19 virus quarantine. First, he travelled from London to visit his parents in the north of England. Then he drove from there into the countryside, in the middle of the lockdown, when everyone else was obliged to self-isolate at home. When the story broke, it dominated the British news media.

'Integrity' is a key value in the British civil service code of conduct for officials, and Sir Bernard Jenkin, chair of the parliamentary committee considering the 'impact and science of Coronavirus', at the very outset of its proceedings challenged Prime Minister Johnson to answer the question, 'Had Cummings broken the code?'[24] There was no response.

In the United Kingdom, the government's programme of legislation is presented annually in the Queens' Speech. On 11 May 2021, it was issued by the prime minister's office and included the proposal to 'strengthen and renew democracy and the constitution' with an 'Electoral Integrity Bill'. Equally, there was a proposal to 'promote the strength and integrity of the union', that is, of the United Kingdom. Not unexpectedly, the proposals were met with a wave of scepticism. For example, it did not take much to imagine the political calculation behind the aspiration to extend voting rights to expats living abroad for more than fifteen years. But there was more than a hint of bravado in giving such prominence to integrity.

Integrity had been headline material for some time. It was only a year since Cummings had been forced to resign for breaking Covid lockdown rules. Johnson himself had been attacked for excessive spending on furnishing his residence. In both cases, it was the word of the accused that was questioned. It prompted the former attorney general Dominic Grieve to speak of an 'integrity vacuum' in government when it was Cummings himself who questioned the prime minister's account that he had paid personally for the redecoration of his Downing Street flat.[25] Integrity vacuum is a striking image, suggesting that a normal political atmosphere is one where we inhale integrity as easily as we do oxygen in the air around us. If only that were the case!

But some may object: What is new in all this? Broken promises, the bung that gains a contract, gunboat diplomacy (admittedly only aimed at French fishing boats) – surely these are the old currency of realpolitik? Isn't this the trademark political realism of the modern age? My answer is there is a profound difference now in the practice of those old dark arts. We can highlight the difference by recalling the writer who defined the realism of the older modern era. Machiavelli came to personify the dark arts of politics for succeeding generations. His prince had often to fight like a beast rather than abide by the law. Not for nothing did he gain the honour, or rather shame, of sharing the name 'Old Nick' with the devil.

In point of fact, despite that reputation, Machiavelli was a serious thinker and commentator on the politics of his day and has exercised a lasting influence on political thought. Regarding our current integrity vacuum, we can recall his many pieces of sound advice to the sixteenth-century ruler, like rewarding faithful servants, avoiding being despised and keeping in touch with the needs of the time.

Machiavelli also proposed that in being a beast, the ruler had to judge the right occasion to imitate the lion or the fox. In the latter case, the prince had to be a great 'feigner or dissembler'. He could retain power by demonstrating every appearance of integrity, 'all faith, all integrity, all humanity and all religion'. But woe betide him if the appearance was the whole reality. Appearances were above all what mattered to the common people, but to be successful the prince often had to act, like the fox, with guile and deception. Always with the proviso, of course, that a switch to the opposite might be necessary.

Clearly, Johnson has been a fighter. Theresa May's fall was nature red in tooth and claw. But did he deceive anyone? Had he the craft of the Renaissance prince in putting on a show of integrity? I suggest that, on the contrary, in this respect he was quite different from the Renaissance prince. Johnson was upfront about what he wanted, quite brazen in changing his mind. He switched sides on Brexit when it suited him.

Johnson's behaviour illustrated the characteristics of the new politics beyond the outdated realism of Machiavelli. Appearances no longer matter. The same applies in the United States. Donald Trump can appear undisturbed by an attempted coup on his behalf, even as it is tracked on live, prime-time television.

The hold Trump retains on a sizeable proportion of those who voted for him in the 2020 election campaign marks another stride beyond integrity. His base of support appears to be strengthened by his recent conviction by a New York court. At the least, a substantial proportion of the public seems unconcerned by the appearance of a lack of integrity. In an assessment of the possible impact of his impending legal trial, Edward Luce of the *Financial Times* pointed to the hold Trump had on the mainstream media.[26] The relatively minor charge he was facing could actually enhance his impunity. Apparently, early data indicated it had increased his popularity among Republican voters. What Johnson and Trump have in common is regard from a large part of the public that seems indifferent even to the lack of pretence of integrity. This is beyond integrity and suggests that charisma is all.

We have arrived at an epochal break that equates with the leap into a new era that the Renaissance experienced. Then, the pretence of integrity became an acceptable stratagem for a ruler. Now power no longer needs moral clothing.

In both the United States and the United Kingdom, a substantial proportion of voters are happy with anyone who uses power to get results. They are largely unmoved, or even intrigued by, flagrant disregard for everyday moral platitudes. They enjoy both grandstanding and an obvious relish for personal aggrandisement. Those who retain their composure and even revel in the widespread disregard for personal integrity will take every advantage of the new conditions. Trump and Johnson have been the supreme practitioners of the new politics of the integrity vacuum. In the empty walls of the vacuum container, the calls for integrity have ever hollower echoes.

8

The Integrity Crisis of Our Time

Of course, the crisis of our time is much bigger than one that simply calls integrity into question. But as we have found all along, integrity is the angle from which we can view the whole picture. Moreover, as we shall see, when it is palpably absent it is then invoked ever more frequently as events unfold.

The West is experiencing a storm that has long been gathering. There are many sides to it, geopolitics, de-globalization, polarization and the growth of populism clustering together, not to mention social media impacts, fake news, racism and mental health. The side I want to focus on is social organization, in particular corporate influence on community and politics.

From the time when Henry Ford founded the assembly line production of the motor vehicle, there has been a continual process of updating industrial production methods, generally known as rationalization.[1] It was paralleled by the growth of state organization, and both contributed to the militarization that led up to the First World War. Bureaucracy became a watchword of the time.[2] This was followed by advances in the study of systems generally by what became known as cybernetics, the science of control, which also prompted feedback into the social sciences.[3]

In the years between the two world wars, western society was in chaos, even in the United States which had not experienced war on its own land. The revered maxims of the Founding Fathers sounded hollow to one who lived through the Great Depression that began in 1929 and lasted through the 1930s. This was Stuart Chase, who after MIT, Harvard and qualifying as an accountant had joined early campaigns against technocracy and become closely linked with the New Deal thinking of Franklin Roosevelt. Chase wrote an article in 1930 that railed against the loss of personal dignity in a vast range of occupations that depended on hiding personal feelings and behaving cravenly to secure a sale, please a boss or endorse a product. Most ordinary Americans had 'betrayed their personal sense of decency and honor' and could not afford 'the luxury of integrity'.[4]

In its scope, Chase's article provided an eloquent anticipation of what was to be a dominant theme of the 1950s in the United States. Integrity was for him living up to the principles that individuals had made their own, and few could afford to do so. He scaled occupations on their integrity: 'Salesmen are low in the scale of integrity, but at least they are alive' (a nice allusion, even if unintended, to the existential aspect of integrity). 'To expect integrity from an elected public servant is almost to expect a miracle.' And, at the bottom, 'certain types of corporation executives'.[5]

Even more prophetic was the way Chase began his article by recalling that one of his assistants was spying on him while he was investigating corporations for the US government. Chase recalled his initial bitterness, and then later pity for a plight that so many Americans shared – 'never has the Republic sunk to lower levels.'[6]

Chase lived through the post-war 'Red Scare' and the McCarthyism of which his anecdote was a striking foretaste. His essay was in so many ways a forerunner of the calls for the new individualism of the 1950s, the pop sociology of

David Riesman, C. Wright Mills and William H. Whyte.[7] There was another side to the calls to resist the encroachments of organizations on individual lives. The corporate world was strengthening its hold on its own fate, becoming increasingly dynamic and expanding. The new issue was to be: Could an organization itself have integrity?

Organizing for integrity

After the Second World War, which had itself stimulated continued applied science for systems, one of the new leading contributors to their analysis was Philip Selznick. His celebrated study of the Tennessee Valley Authority (TVA) became a benchmark contribution to the new science of organizations.[8] The key activity of the TVA when it was established under Franklin Roosevelt's New Deal of the 1930s was to assist agriculture through the extension of electric power in the valley.

But there was a multiplier effect on the life of the valley, as the Extension Services of the land-grant colleges in seven states became the effective delivery agents for the agricultural program. Education then morphed into social action, and the Authority itself absorbed an ideological commitment.[9]

Selznick followed up the theoretical issues in his study with what must count as one of the most provocative assertions of intellectual independence ever, or, if one likes, intellectual integrity. He took as a benchmark for what he called organizational 'character' the 'distinctive competence' of the Bolshevik Party (more than an oxymoron, anathema!).[10] As with the TVA, he found a continuing process of modifying a past heritage, in this case older socialist parties whose members had to be re-educated to new capabilities, quite unlike what was demanded of members of regular political parties.[11]

In this character formation of an organization, Selznick found the role of leaders in commitment to values to be the central issue. It was here that he identified the defence of institutional integrity as one of four key tasks for the leader. The others were definition of the institutional mission and role, its embodiment of purpose and the ordering of conflict. With values, it was not just a matter of survival, but their maintenance as part of the distinctive identity of the organization, but there was always a problem where values were tenuous or insecure. In his account of leadership, Selznick wrote, 'Few aspects of organization are so important, yet so badly neglected by students of the subject, as this problem of institutional integrity.'[12]

Burnishing his maverick credentials even further, Selznick went on to propose that it was actually elite autonomy within the organization that was a necessary requirement to sustain its values. As another human artefact, the organization equally could be judged by the criterion of its integrity. But it took the efforts of some, for whom its identity as a whole was their responsibility, to safeguard its special values. Elite responsibility was the only way to solve rivalry between subordinate units which were defending 'the integrity of their functions'.[13]

In this incidental allusion to the integrity of the work entrusted to sections of an organization, Selznick is opening recognition of the way the pursuit of integrity can be a potent source of conflict as much as the realization of values. Moreover, it can arise at any level in an organization. The maintenance staff, the cleaners, the porters can all care for the integrity of their work.

Higher education institutions are a prime example of this potential for conflict between parties proclaiming their own integrity. There you have at least three sites of integrity that compete to assert what their advocates consider most important for their own fulfilment. There are the students who are finding identity and purpose in the wider society as well as seeking qualifications; there are the academics who are committed to the advance of knowledge in their field; and there are those who have the administrative responsibility to maintain the institution on which both academics and students depend.

It is therefore no surprise when regular conflicts arise between these three groups signalling their own integrity. For one American academic with a big public profile, Stanley Fish, those conflicts are only to be solved if each group gets on with the task formally assigned to it within the university as a whole. He targeted particularly academics who allowed their commitment to wider public causes to influence their work in the classroom. He argued, 'Sometimes the danger to institutional integrity comes from academics themselves when they try to bend the university to a political purpose.'[14]

Fish gives as an example the case of the Southern Methodist University (SMU) contemplating the establishment of the George W. Bush Presidential Library on its campus. There was a predictable uproar within the academic community where some, among other things, pointed to the university's code of ethics that included 'Integrity in work' along with 'Pursuit of truth', 'Respect for persons', 'Responsible use of resources', and 'Accountability'.

Fish was scathing. The moral yardstick did not mean the university was protecting its integrity. Rather, it was forsaking its integrity when it made judgements that belonged 'to the electorate and history'.[15] His contribution to the uproar over the SMU proposal (subsequently approved) echoed years of debate from the post-war years of the counterculture onwards. Could the study of social criticism be excluded from the curriculum?

The sharp lines Fish seeks to establish within the university community themselves depend on an account of integrity that finds its realization in the mutual exclusivity of values. He is expressing the compartmentalization of life in the ever more specialized occupational structures of our time. Is that to be a no-go area for serious academic research?

Corporate scandals

In the twenty-first century, the issues raised by Chase, Selznick and Fish have had headline repercussions far beyond those they imagined. At the very beginning of the Bush Jr presidency, the worst corporate scandal in American history broke with the bankruptcy of an energy company by the name of Enron. Only five years before, it had been declared by *Fortune* magazine to be the country's most innovative company.[16]

It began as a regular oil pipeline laying firm, but from 1985 chief executive Kenneth Lay worked tirelessly to turn it into an energy-trading business that for a time was the seventh-largest corporation in America. But it was all based on fraudulent accounting. Lay was convicted of fraud and conspiracy in 2006. He died before sentence could be announced.

The events that led to the collapse of Enron were precipitated by the disclosures of one of its staff turned whistle-blower, Sherron Watkins. Trained originally with the major accountancy firm Arthur Andersen, she became a vice-president of Enron in 1997, but found huge unreported losses in a fake entity called Raptor. She had challenged Lay in a letter in 2001, writing, 'I am incredibly nervous that we will implode in a wave of accounting scandals.'[17]

In the same issue of the *New York Times*, where the letter was published, its author was given front-page treatment with reporters tracking down colleagues and neighbours. One of them described her as an active Christian and morally sound, and a former Enron executive said, 'I have never heard anyone question her judgment, her integrity and her veracity.'[18]

Watkins's letter to Lay was both detailed about specific accounting flaws and ready to point to general issues applying to the whole profession. She wrote, 'The overriding basic principle of accounting is that if you explain the "accounting treatment" to a man in the street, would you influence his investment decision? Would he sell or buy the stock based on a thorough understanding of the facts?'[19] Such an 'overriding basic principle' was exercising the firm that had audited Enron's accounts, Arthur Andersen. As a result, they felt bound to fire a partner who had ordered the destruction of thousands of documents and emails once the official investigation into Enron had begun. The accounting firm's managing partner claimed Enron management had deceived it, but also admitted, 'The integrity of this firm is in question. Our reputation is our most important asset.'[20] There was a history of problem accounting with the firm already, and in August 2002 it ceased to operate. The big five accounting firms in the world were reduced to four, and they remain at that number to this day.

If anyone imagines such scandals could only affect the biggest capitalist country of all time, then Europe has tried hard to show it too can match it in dodgy accounting. In July 2020, the London-based *Financial Times* (*FT*) ran a full-page article 'Time to audit the auditors'.[21] The reason was the insolvency announced on 25 June 2020 of Wirecard, a major German-based financial services provider and payments processor. Its share valuation touched €24 billion in 2018.

Once again, it appears that reported balances simply did not exist, on this occasion €1.9 billion. The *FT* reported that the auditors, EY, had relied on bogus documentation. But it also quoted Professor Karthik Ramanna of the Oxford Blavatnik School of Government saying, 'The integrity of the cash account is totally central to the whole system of double-entry bookkeeping. If there is no integrity to the cash account, then the whole system is just a joke.'[22]

In fact, it was the *FT* which had uncovered the scandal through a five-year investigation led by its reporter Dan McCrum. In writing up the story, he told how his enquiries were met by the German press with accusations that all was in order and that he was a criminal. Meanwhile, a source was saying Wirecard would pay $10 million to stop writing about them.[23]

The story runs on and on. The German audit watchdog imposed 'unprecedented sanctions' on EY but it would appear that the whole case could still run on for many years. No decision has yet been reached on the civil and criminal liabilities that the firm might incur as a result of its involvement with Wirecard.[24] According to one report, the firm is 'facing an avalanche of lawsuits'.[25]

The most recent dramatic episode in the Wirecard saga at the time of writing concerns its former chief operating officer, Jan Marsalek. He is thought to be living in Moscow and has been named as a contact for five Bulgarians who have been charged in London with spying for Russia.[26] The latest information is that he has been named in a warrant issued by the Austrian police, and that evidence is mounting that Wirecard was being used as a shadow financial network to pay for Russian undercover operations in Europe and Africa.[27]

Corporate wrongdoing in Germany on a major scale was also revealed in relation to its major motor vehicle manufacturer, Volkswagen. Over more than five years, diesel fuel-emissions control systems only worked for testing in laboratories and were blocked for normal driving. Subsequently so-called emissions defeat devices have been found in multiple car makers in different countries for both diesel and non-diesel vehicles.[28]

But of all the corporate scandals, the most egregious must be the one that finally hit the headlines in the United Kingdom, but only after the appearance of a television series based on events that extended over a twenty-year period. This scandal has an international aspect in that it involved the British public body, the Post Office, and the Japanese technology company Fujitsu. Fujitsu was responsible for installing an online computerized accounting system, Horizon, to be used for the day-to-day monetary transactions in post offices. Any discrepancies between what the system registered and how much money was received over the counter had to be rectified by post office staff through paying for deficits out of their own income. Fujitsu guaranteed that the Horizon system was tamperproof, and over the years the Post Office either dismissed and/or pursued criminal charges against its staff arising out of Horizon accounting statements. More than seven hundred were punished, some jailed, and in four cases staff committed suicide. But over the years evidence mounted that the Horizon system was faulty and that, despite denials, its results could be subject to human intervention.

The enormity of the scandal was all the greater given that very strong evidence of problems with the prosecutions had been published in the investigative (and humorous) journal *Private Eye* as far back as September 2011, and followed up on repeated occasions thereafter. It was only when a television series caused a public outcry that the British government ordered a public inquiry.[29] There had been systematic denial of any problems from every responsible level in the Post Office. The latest twist to the story is that the Conservative government brought forward legislation to exonerate all those punished for false accounting in post offices during the period of Horizon's use. Compensation is still only at an early stage.

Enron, Wirecard and the UK Post Office scandals are all instances of corporate behaviour where the blame for any potential illegality extends far beyond any one individual, the 'bad apple' in a basket of good fruit. At the very least in each case, dozens if not hundreds of employees have been complicit, either directly as accomplices or as silent witnesses to behaviour with far-reaching damaging consequences for the wider society. Turning a blind eye can be the beginning of a long road leading to corporate corruption.

The failure here was not proactive, the quest for advantage, but neglect of due care for the interests of employees or the public. There were too many who gained from the lapse in standards for anyone to risk standing out against injustice. They simply turned the other way. Similar cases of endemic

failure in the past in the United Kingdom include the con-
taminated blood scandal where between 1970 and the 1990s
around 30,000 people were given blood infected with hepatitis
C or HIV. Another such instance was the Windrush scandal
when a hostile environment to immigration declared by Prime
Minister May, plus the laxity of officials, combined in 2018
to initiate deportation for people who had arrived legally in
the United Kingdom from Caribbean countries as long ago as
1973.

Each case shows how the personal integrity of an individual
is exposed to risk in an organization with repercussions that
still have not received satisfactory resolution. What these
instances have in common is an organizational climate where
too many are complicit in denial that anything wrong has happened. The blame for inaction within the culpable organization
spreads so widely that the risk to anyone's career in it through
exposing it is too great. Those who take the risk are popularly
known as whistle-blowers, and there have been attempts to
entrench their rights in law.[30]

In a broad-ranging polemic against the big entities, states
and corporations that dominate the modern economy, David
Runciman (2023) has singled out the monopoly power of the
tech companies where their own search engines provide the
data that justify the advertising fees they charge. He also finds
that their ownership structure, while involving shareholders,
often guarantees control by the original founder. For instance,
Mark Zuckerberg has a majority voting stake in Meta, even
though he owns only 13 per cent of the shares.[31]

When the power of artificial intelligence (AI) is added to
the armoury of the big beasts, then the possibility of a future
shaped and controlled by corporate entities looms, and beyond
that the autonomy of AI in controlling the corporate world,
and hence the fate of humankind. The most exotic of science
fiction fantasies now come nearer to being possible future
dystopias.

Runciman wraps up all past developments like the scientific and industrial revolutions, capitalism and globalization in the term 'the first singularity', all facilitated by states and corporations of the modern world, 'artificial agents' as he calls them. The 'second' arrives when the agents that shaped those processes adopt AI, and indeed they have the common characteristic of being beyond individual control. We move then into the era of the AI state.[32]

Governance for integrity

Company governance matters for the whole system right the way down to how it records its transactions. That certainly was the case with Enron and Arthur Andersen. The integrity of the corporation then also depends on rules – standards of procedure that it observes and that others can rely on. In contemporary societies the public legal system provides those guarantees.

In the United States, the President's Council on Integrity and Efficiency (PCIE) and the Executive Council on Integrity and Efficiency (ECIE) were set up in May 1992 by George H. W. Bush. They were effectively combined in the Council of the Inspectors General on Integrity and Efficiency (CIGIE) in the Inspector General Reform Act of October 2008. Thus both enhancements of the prominence of integrity for US government came during Bush presidencies, and both father and son made integrity part of their public persona.

In the United Kingdom, lawyer John Bowers has called the patchwork of bodies that govern standards in public life an '"integrity branch" of constitutional governance ("a Fifth Estate")'. Their overall inspiration was provided by the Nolan Committee set up by Prime Minister John Major in 1994 which established Seven Principles of Public Life.[33]

The second principle was integrity: 'Holders of public office must avoid placing themselves under any obligation to people or organizations that might try inappropriately to influence them in their work. They should not act or take decisions in order to gain financial or other material benefits for themselves, their family, or their friends. They must declare or resolve any interests or relationships.'[34] For Bowers, it provides ample justification to document innumerable subsequent breaches of integrity in British public life.[35]

The rules governing firms in the West may be set by law-making authorities or by associations that make membership dependent on following their rules. An example of the former is the draft directive of the Council of Ministers of the European Union on 7 October 2003, aiming to establish high level principles for the supervision of investment firms with two main purposes:

1   to enhance the protection of investors and market integrity; and
2   to further the promotion of fair, transparent, efficient and integrated financial markets.

Another example comes from the business sector. It aims to enhance the knowledge base necessary to service markets. Originating in an agreement between American financial analysts in 1947, a non-profit organization, the Chartered Financial Analyst Institute now has a code of conduct and more than one hundred and fifty member societies worldwide. It provides examinations to qualify for its prestigious Chartered Financial Analyst (CFA) award. It also monitors ethical standards in the global investment management industry.

The long-standing managing director of its Standards and Financial Market Integrity division, Kurt Schacht, has drawn attention to the significance of expert networks for many years. He advances the claims of his Institute's Asset Manager Code of Professional Conduct to give investors 'new reason to believe in the integrity of markets'.[36]

Market movements have become an ever more esoteric sphere with the development of high-frequency trading (HFT). Trading can happen in microseconds following computerized transaction programmes. The resulting market outcomes are only predictable in principle by those who design the programmes. The very speed of the transactions, based in vast accumulations of data, provides little in the way of paper evidence. When the Securities and Exchange Commission sought to explain the 6 May crash, it took them five months to produce a report. None of this helps market confidence.[37]

The question arises, then, to what extent can integrity shape markets?[38] Let us return to one of the most celebrated statements by the most famous of economists of all time, Adam Smith: 'It is not from the benevolence of the butcher, the brewer or the baker that we expect our dinner, but from their regard for their own interest.' It is contained in one short chapter where he explains the basis of the division of labour, that those tradesmen are each able to exchange the surplus of their productive efforts with others.[39]

Interests are key, and the extent of the market in which they can be satisfied is limited only by the means of communication. Historically, Smith explained water was a great facilitator of commerce, with the Nile, the Ganges and the great rivers of China. We can amplify that theme by drawing on the work of the pioneering Peruvian economist Hernando de Soto, who looks behind exchange to property and the stunted capacity to realize the value of undocumented property in the underdeveloped world. Knowledge, too, is a prerequisite for market participation.[40]

Both authorities, Adam Smith and de Soto, imply that the principle of markets is that they are free of limits beyond any that nature or human frailty may impose. That is the principle that Max Weber endorsed too in his famous distinction between open and closed relationships. The market is open to anyone, unless restrictions are imposed that limit it to certain people or forbid certain kinds of behaviour.

Ultimately, a market establishes itself on trust and the proven reliability of the participants. But the market itself? It is beyond integrity, even though sites of integrity may be established in it. It is like society, landscapes, weather or space, something that always escapes beyond the islands of control we establish within it. Markets are in principle inherently open and consequently lack the ring-fencing that is a key criterion of integrity. Efforts to supply the fences are an ongoing process, but digital developments continually outstrip them.[41]

In the rising interest in codes and rules to cover every aspect of life, we have a reconstruction of what was once an open area for public debate and decision making. The public sphere is now indistinguishable from governance, and in that more and more the experts are the lawyers. Judges in a legal system have the burden, and occasionally the benefit, of being the persons to whom society at large attributes the greatest degree of integrity.

In the case of legal systems, we have the prototype of modern institutional integrity and equally the cardinal distinction between judge and person that is the foundational model for role distinctions in modern society. With Lord Chancellor Francis Bacon, we saw in chapter 2 the birth pangs of the new modernity in his career even as he was recognizing the future of applied scientific knowledge.[42]

Bacon's assertion of the essential quality of integrity for judges remains as true today as in James I's time. In both interpretation and application, the personal beliefs and interests of the judge are expected to be entirely irrelevant, excluded and unquestionable. Indeed, that defines the integrity of the judge, alongside unimpeachable knowledge of the law. But political pressures on judges are an inevitable risk. This was the case in the United Kingdom at the end of 2017 in the run-up to the final vote in Parliament on leaving the European Union.

The government of Theresa May had hoped to leave the European Union without further need to seek Parliament's approval. When three High Court judges ruled against the government, those newspapers that had always been vociferous advocates for Brexit were outraged by the decision, with one of them denouncing the judges as 'enemies of the people'.[43] Two days after the ruling, the Lord Chancellor, Liz Truss, felt bound to defend the independence of the judiciary as the 'foundation upon which our rule of law is built', adding, 'The reputation of our judiciary is unrivalled the world over.'[44]

Actually, the worldwide reputation that Truss mentions is not just imperial nostalgia. It has real consequences for the British judicial system. Russian oligarchs found the United Kingdom a hospitable place until recently.[45] 'Exporting Integrity' was a leading article headline in the *Financial Times*. It welcomed the financial success of the courts but pointed to the risk that a service for rich foreigners might squeeze out help for the average English citizen at a time when legal aid was being cut back.[46]

Clearly, the system in its entirety, not just individual judges, is subject to the integrity test. Moreover, that test is never passed once and for all time. Changing circumstances, not just economic and political events, bring integrity into question. The digital age has consequences for every aspect of daily life and public institutions.[47]

Bowers has proposed possible overarching alternative bodies, such as an Ethics Commission to regulate standards throughout government, yet he makes no mention of AI. The continuing focus on integrity in western institutions is a function of the rapidity of technological change and the general advance in rationalization. The globalization of the economy in particular brings change into the everyday lives of citizens and is reflected in populism. It is there that integrity enters into public discourse and surfaces in the media frenzies of our previous chapter.

Integrity in peril

The Corruption Perceptions Index (CPI) for 2022 from Transparency International, the civil society group dedicated to exposing corruption worldwide, shows a decline in perceived freedom from corruption in most western countries, including the United Kingdom. The United States ranks below the United Kingdom (24th as against 18th of 180 countries) but has improved since 2021. More extensive exposure of corruption in the West shows its declining difference from the rest. But the decline of its more comprehensive institutional integrity indicates its ever-growing absorption into the wider culture of a globalized world.

The CPI measures perceptions of corruption in the public sector. But the western crisis is one of confidence in its institutions generally, and that includes business, education, science and civil society more generally. The collapse of integrity in British public life has much more to do with the chaotic procedures in bodies and institutions that had previously been taken for granted in everyday life. The lack of integrity in the British National Health Service results from its failure to fulfil performance standards like waiting times for treatment, not from endemic dishonesty. Indeed, the public sees its long-suffering staff as victims of the system. It is the crumbling of an entity that was once integral to British life that provokes public anger.[48]

Threats to institutional integrity can also come from those who are placed in positions intended to safeguard it. This is the case with electoral registration laws in many states in the United States. Each state has its own ID requirements for voting. Historically, these have been a persistent focus for controversy as they can be contrived to have a deterrent effect on those who would be most likely to vote against the sitting representatives. For instance, in 2013, North Dakota passed House Bill 1332 to exclude anyone from voting without a permanent address, the main target group being Native Americans.

Nicholas Allen and Sarah Birch (2015) have pointed to the growing decline of trust in politicians in both the United States and the United Kingdom. They concluded this on the basis of thorough empirical research into public attitudes. This was in the mid-2010s. Now everything points to a continuing decline. Moreover, it is embedded in a wider loss of confidence in western institutions and in public and corporate bodies generally. It all amounts to the integrity crisis of the West.

A decade ago, near the end of the year 2013, more than five hundred leading writers published an open letter for the whole world to see. They began by pointing to the capacity for mass surveillance now in the hands of states and corporations. They ended with a call to those bodies to respect the rights of individuals and to control the use of their personal data. Correspondingly, they called on citizens to defend those rights, on the United Nations to create an international bill of rights, and on governments to sign up to it.[49] The premise for the call was contained in the second paragraph. It runs as follows: 'The basic pillar of democracy is the inviolable integrity of the individual. Human integrity extends beyond the physical body. In their thoughts and in their personal environments and communications all individuals have the right to remain unobserved and unmolested.' The very next sentence of the following paragraph begins, 'This fundamental human right . . .' There are six paragraphs explaining how surveillance infringes integrity. They aim to set a right to control personal data in the contemporary frame of the digital age, technology and democracy. In effect, they assert that the clash of surveillance and integrity must be the new focus for political concern in our time.

The capacity for covert observation of individual behaviour is vastly enhanced by digital technology. But even enhanced state surveillance may not be the major threat that our writers of the open letter portray. According to sociologist Shoshana Zuboff, its use by the giant technology corporations to engineer human experience turns it into 'surveillance capitalism'. In so doing, they 'disregard . . . the moral integrity of the autonomous individual'.[50]

If it is in connections between things that the idea of integrity demonstrates its strength, it also means it stretches ever more widely, even as things and their connections do. The sheer acceleration in the rate of change in contemporary life means that integrity is invoked and dismissed just as rapidly, and the focus of our attention shifts from one provocative instance to another.

We attended to a pivotal moment in the western history when Machiavelli gave intellectual recognition to the realities of power politics and ushered in what came to be called realism in the affairs of state ever since. The pretence, not the possession of integrity, was one incidental aspect of that radical shift. It was of course part of the wider cultural transformation of the time when stage performance became the medium for leading ideas in public discourse and when a wider audience could access the language that hitherto had echoed only in the chambers of royalty and aristocracy.

We are witnessing now just such a shift, as the public sphere is now located in both mass and social communication media, and the integrity of performance in the media can supplant any consideration of the personal reality behind it. The difference from the place of integrity in the old realism is profound but also subtle. Machiavelli's prince pretended to have integrity, but his performance purported to represent himself. Because it was pretence, the observer was to be deceived into thinking this was the real thing.

In the case of the media presence of the public figures of today, and especially of those with the prominence of a Trump or a Johnson, integrity of the person no longer prevails as a key component of their political appeal. They don't have to pretend to be the kind of person that they are not. Their appearance on screen is an act, which may or may not have the integrity of 'good viewing' or 'looking the part', but it has no inherent or necessary relationship with the actor as a whole person. They have the celebrity status accorded to actors of the Jacobean stage, a status that first gained political power in the twentieth century in the person of Ronald Reagan.[51]

Perhaps it is only right and just to give the last word on the merging of public interest in stage drama and politics to the journalist who has been deeply involved in reporting the Wirecard scandal for the *Financial Times*. Sam Jones reflects on his time in Vienna, seeing the rise of investigative theatre, being reminded of the play in 1914 by the Viennese satirist, Karl Kraus, *The Last Days of Mankind*: 'people seem to become trapped in performance, actors without agency in a story over which they have no control.'[52]

Conclusion:
Integrity for the Human Future

This book has shown how, through the ages, integrity has been an inspiration, guide and accompaniment to so many western achievements, to creativity and innovation. It has been a unique feature of western development. It has been linked through the centuries with the work or names of its exemplary persons, such as William Shakespeare, Benjamin Franklin, Jane Austen and George Orwell. It has motivated and shaped the reform of governmental and corporate institutions. It has been the clarion call for the election of an American president.

If there are words that can change history, then integrity has a claim to be one. But even as it has marshalled an army of virtues and called for commitment to them, it has equally highlighted a negative side. We have seen how its very absence has led recently to the declaration of an integrity vacuum in British politics.[1]

Currently on both sides of the Atlantic, those same political uproars and public scandals where integrity is cited might suggest it is just as well adapted to accompany the decline of the West, to track the dissolution of institutions, the escape of technology from human control, the rise of populist demagoguery. Those are reasons why we must pause and take stock.

First, we ought to ask what the so-called decline of the West amounts to. Does it mean that its past achievements amount to nothing in a globalized world? Could the idea of integrity suffer the same challenges as ideas like liberal democracy and the rule of law? We need to take account of how the idea of integrity has survived into this chaotic present time, and if it is making a difference in the West now, ask whether it can contribute to a new world order in the same way.

On the decline of the West, we need to understand this is old news, indeed at least a century old since its most famous announcement by Oswald Spengler.[2] Writing immediately after the defeat of Germany in the First World War, he described the West as just one particular civilization in world history, and like all civilizations doomed ultimately to die.

Spengler's forebodings have never been altogether forgotten. Forty years after him, the greatest western historian of civilization, Arnold Toynbee, summed up his twelve-volume study of history with a rejoinder to Spengler, pointing to an ecumenical civilization that the West had begun, but where one could expect the non-western to break through. I think, however, even he would be surprised at the subsequent absorption of the West into this wider world.[3]

Alvin Toffler, writing in the wake of environmental pessimism of the 1970s, mentioned the post-Second World War guru of American foreign policy, Henry Kissinger (now the late), speaking 'in Spenglerian accents about the decline of the West'.[4] To my mind, Toffler's book *The Third Wave* best took the pulse of the time by writing of civilization as belonging to human society as a whole. He was describing an economic and technological transformation affecting every society. It was a book beyond geopolitics.[5]

Our own world is also beyond geopolitics, though you might not know it from media headlines, when the wars in Ukraine and Gaza involve Russia and the United States respectively, and when the United States and China meet as partners to discuss maintaining mutual security communication relations. But the underlying changes in our lives amount to a technological and social transformation that goes far beyond episodic military conflicts, however dangerous they may be, and even though their outcome might be a nuclear holocaust ending civilization as we know it. We just have to think of the digital computing advances, of the World Wide Web, of social media and now generative artificial intelligence (also a potential existential threat to our species). These are the communication technologies of global society.

Their initial thrust all came from the West, its gift to the rest, or perhaps rather, the long-delayed payment for two centuries of imperial exploitation. Whatever the moral balance sheet, the outcome in ties between people everywhere means we are all in it together, whatever the fate of this world. Those bonds cannot be broken, even by so-called de-globalization. But is this the decline of the West?

I prefer to call it an 'unwinding'.[6] This conveys the sense of a dispersion of products, skills and tastes that have originated in the West but have been disseminated worldwide. They are tied to technologies but are based in use and understanding beyond borders. This has been the case with technologies since time immemorial.[7] Once invented, they become the common property of humankind.

But this is not the same with products of an immaterial kind – ideas, customs, artefacts that belong to the historical experience of a people. They are often guarded jealously for many different reasons, the rarity of a crop, the sacredness of a place, the uniqueness of a work of art. And this applies in spades to language.

The great English philosopher John Locke, who remains the authoritative voice of English empiricism and a matter-of-fact approach to the world around us, had no doubts about the limits of cross-cultural communication. Understanding in one's own language was a complex enough process that he examined in depth, but translation of even ordinary terms to another language would find almost no exact equivalent.[8]

We observed early on that only very few languages have a word directly descended from the Latin for integrity. They are, with a few exceptions such as Romanian, based in Western Europe. Neighbouring countries have borrowed at a later date, as with German and Polish, but still make no regular use of the foreign import. Even in the United Kingdom, the Welsh language has neither an equivalent, nor borrows the term from its next-door neighbour. As for Chinese – well, it's from another world.

But of course, English is now, more than any other, the world language, and therefore access to the idea of integrity is open to any educated reader anywhere. More to the point, we might quite reasonably ask: Can the idea of integrity, embroiled as it is in the chaos and integrity vacuum of today's West, possibly survive in our globalized world? To answer that, we should recall its course of development over the last two millennia.

We can remind ourselves of its mundane origin in ancient Rome, in the Latin *integritas*, a reference to the completeness and undamaged quality of any entity whatsoever, along with the standards that ensured that condition. As such, it could refer to things of all kinds, from food to earthenware, from buildings to persons, and in the latter case it could refer to moral qualities.[9]

That origin extended to customs repellent to our feelings today. It reflected the objectification of women, as male property. The virgin girl's hymen had to be unbroken before marriage in ancient Rome, and loss of its *integritas*, its intactness, could result in death inflicted by her owner, her father. But this linkage of the completeness of any object, whether human or not, to the standards that made it complete became fundamental for the later development of the concept of integrity.

In effect, this bonding of two highly abstract concepts, completeness of an entity combined with the standards that ensure its existence, is evidence of an intuitive understanding of a foundational feature of our human existence that was to have huge later significance. It was to become a distinguishing feature of western discourse about the place of human beings in the world around them. It directed attention into the composition and durability of any object whatsoever, and that included people as well as the things we make.

Other cultures appreciate high standards, in art as well as in people. We only need to recall the Confucian *junzi*, the superior man, a man of many talents. But the word 'integrity' implies much more than evaluative standards. It has a generalized application across all objects, human, natural, artefactual and all their associated qualities. It makes survival, lasting existence, dependent on principles and standards that inhere in the entity.

Moreover, in the linkage between the entity and the standards it embodies, integrity effectively grasps what has been recognized as the distinctive and foundational feature of the human experience, namely the development of culture and cultures. In other words, it anticipates something that only came close to full recognition in the West in the eighteenth century when the idea of culture in the sense we use it today became current.[10]

We now are fully aware of the fact that we largely create the world we inhabit. We do it first by shaping materials based in our understanding of the principles that govern all matter. Second, we direct our own activities by sharing our intimations of what is right and wrong, valuable and worthless, with other people. As a result, the products of human creative activities are all around us and we live in the heritage from our past.

Integrity as a value is a permanent reminder that we have made our past, that the future depends on our choices and new directions are always possible. Moreover, just as the technologies that have developed in the West are now worldwide properties, is it unthinkable that an idea which has so often accompanied innovation and creative work might also travel with them?

The idea of integrity has developed over two millennia from those elementary, often crude beginnings and continues to do so. In the account up to now we have seen how its application has extended to phenomena as diverse as the text of *Animal Farm* and the American Council of the Inspectors General on Integrity and Efficiency. If that is any indication of the versatility of the idea, then its continuing use beyond the bounds of the West is more than simply credible.

Here I think we can draw some confidence from John Locke, for he held that knowledge of general principles is not inborn but acquired through reason and experience. Even if they are not observed at all times, their understanding is accessible to all. In his words, 'They are equally true, though not equally evident.' 'Justice and truth are the common ties of society' and even 'outlaws and robbers' have to 'keep faith' among themselves.[11]

Now, in the case of integrity we have an idea that expresses recognition of the relation between principles and existence. It arrives early in western thought, but there is no reason to think that it is an idea inaccessible to reason elsewhere in the world. It has accompanied transformation in the West, but it hasn't been copyrighted!

Let us hold fast to the unique intuition that underlies the concept. This is that human beings are both physical bodies and driven by values. Their bodies exist in a material world and obey its laws. Their values can only be realized in that world, but they come from outside it. But when we say 'outside it', where is this 'outside' of the material world? Traditionally, it was held to be the spiritual, and the pair material/spiritual was the axis around which speculation about eternity, life's purpose and God's design revolved before modern science displaced theology from the popular imagination.

Today, in the secularized West, 'spirit' as a term survives in attenuated form in expressions like 'team spirit', suggesting there is more to the success of a football team than just the sum of the talents of its individual players.[12] Very broadly, we can say that today 'culture' is the western substitute for 'spirit'. The idea of culture has become the contemporary bearer of all those intangible but effective elements in life that carry our identities, plans, hopes and fears forward into the future.

In the humanities and social sciences, culture has become an all-encompassing concept, including ideas and values, customs and styles of expression, creative products, both popular and elite, and very broadly ways of living, as well as our imaginations of what could be otherwise. But culture also invades and shapes the material world. The objects familiar in our daily lives, the plants, the food and the utensils, are solid enough, yet we also recognize them as imports from other cultures, the oranges from Spain, the spaghetti from Italy, the chopsticks from China.

However, linking these products with national entities itself puts artificial boundaries around culture, for orange cultivation extends far beyond Spain and chopsticks belong to Eastern Asia as a whole. Moreover, increasingly we recognize that so much of what was once regarded as specific to a national or regional culture is now part of world culture, sometimes loosely called global culture.[13]

The interlocking of the material and the cultural is a fundamental feature of human life on this planet. Indeed, it distinguishes what is human from the rest of creation. Of all our abstract concepts that guide our lives, integrity is the most prominent in combining those two sides of human existence, the material or physical on the one hand, the cultural or spiritual on the other. It focuses on the complete, distinct and durable features of any object and makes those depend on observing fundamental rules that reach far beyond its distinct existence. In these respects, it applies to natural objects obeying laws that scientists discover and define. It relates then to our physiology as much as to our morality.

To gain an idea of its future prospect in worldwide society, I will highlight what I consider the three great transitions when integrity's scope has expanded far beyond its origin, without ever departing from its Janus-like aspect, its foundational double-sidedness. Each jump forward has involved a significant expansion of its field of reference. Each has run concurrently with, and been integral to, profound transformations in the West. We will consider the three in turn.

The triumph of Christianity in the later Roman Empire was the beginning of fundamental change in Europe.[14] For us today, integrity equated with virginity is repellent, but from a beginning with such a crude aspect developed an idea that became profoundly important for the medieval Christian Church.

Embedded in Christianity's elaborate theology was a moral code that was to impose burdensome, and in the event, impossible demands on its clergy. It extended the scope of integrity beyond virginity to chastity in general, and was even more stringent for men than for women. The priesthood was exclusively male and required complete obedience to the Church's authority, as well as observing its strict instructions on chastity.

Furthermore, at the same time, the Christian belief system absorbed the ancient atomistic outlook that maintained the world was made of things. To that it added something quite distinct, but just as fundamental. In place of the Roman pantheon of gods with a distinct presence, personalities and powers, the Christians, like their Jewish forerunners, put their faith in a single supreme God who had created this whole world, all the things the Romans knew and much more besides.

Linkage to a belief in an almighty creator God initiated the **first** of integrity's three great extensions of scope after its origin in ancient Rome. Integrity became intimately connected with creation from then on. Integrity applied to all things, and it was God who had created them all. What men did with those things after their creation was a matter between them and Him.

The whole medieval period for Europe proved to be decisive in shaping what was later to be known as the West. A division of the Christian Church between West and East meant that Latin became the language for clergy under the authority of the Roman papacy. Its terminology seeped into the vernaculars of the territories west of the Rhine. Centuries of Christian domination of both political and everyday life brought with them the acceptance of a worldview where the presence or absence of integrity in things and people was a taken-for-granted feature of judgements on what was praiseworthy or repugnant in normal life.

The **second** of the great transitions came with the Western Renaissance and Reformation. Those movements were accompanied by both the rediscovery of classical literature and the flourishing of the vernacular languages of Western Europe: integrity, *integrité, integrità, integridad,* all words taking forward that original double-sidedness of the Latin word. It was in the west of Europe, where Roman Catholicism had kept it alive, that the heritage of the Latin language had its greatest influence.

Once the Roman Church had lost its exclusive hold on Western European Christianity, integrity began to flourish too as a secular concept. The rise of Protestantism not only broke the hold of the Catholic clergy, it also brought the believer into a direct relation with the creator God. Three centuries later, according to the Scottish writer Thomas Carlyle (1795–1881), 'Protestantism is the grand root from which our whole subsequent European History branches out.'[15]

From the fifteenth to the seventeenth centuries, integrity blossomed as a concept, its pretence being part of the armoury of Machiavelli's prince and its observance the professional pride of Bacon's judge. With both of those very different appreciations of the potential of the integrity idea came a further fundamental expansion of its scope. It was now a summation of behaviour distinct from the personality of the one who acted it out. The devious prince and the judge had this in common. They were both performing.

That made integrity a fertile source of inspiration for the stage, too. For Shakespeare chastity, hence integrity for women in his plays, had begun to be a sign of their power, control of their bodies, corresponding too to the popular image of the 'virgin' queen, Elizabeth I. His *Cymbeline* evoked the most ancient archetype in his woman resisting all assaults on her honour and culminating in the restoration of empire and peace in Europe.

A very few years later, integrity crossed the Atlantic Ocean with the Pilgrim Fathers as an inspiration to the ancestors of those who went on to found the United States. The impetus it gave to self-assertion and creativity spurred the American settlers to build new communities, to invent new things and foster the capitalist spirit. Integrity became the talisman for the Founding Fathers of the new republic.

The **third** great transition is in our own time.[16] We have seen how integrity shapes public debate, governs the aspirations of scientists and writers, inspires the establishment of public bodies, inhabits codes of behaviour for officials, becomes the focus of enquiries into the collective behaviour of corporate bodies and of their employees and is disregarded by political leaders, prompting denunciation of our political vacuum. If it is the emblem of western public life, it is also its scourge.

But the image of the integrity vacuum is not even the most colourful description of the behaviour of public figures in our time. They appear to benefit from a general acknowledgement that we cannot expect those in power to follow rules. A general exemption for them from standards and principles that govern 'ordinary' people in everyday life seems to be a regular expectation. The Renaissance ruler's pretence is no longer necessary.

Richard Sennett has described the processes at work that result in this situation as 'charisma becoming uncivilized', and linked it directly to the importance of twentieth-century electronic media in creating a compulsive interest in personality. As far as politics is concerned, that means paradoxically that the politician's job, producing political outcomes, is less important than what is projected on the screen. Sennett comments that it is misleadingly facile to call this an act: 'What is believable about the politician are his motives, his sentiments, his "integrity".'[17]

Yet it is closer in kind to the integrity we saw with Tom Driberg, proud of his vices and fully appreciated by his friends. 'Authenticity' better describes the aspiration of the contemporary politician. 'Warts and all' makes for a real person, and the public, or at least a section of it, can warm to her, or him (usually), as a result. So much then of our public life is beyond integrity.

As we know, the antics of a Donald Trump or a Boris Johnson are not without consequences. After all, they did each become leaders of their respective countries. They both illustrate the continuing, indeed possibly expanding, influence of personality and media image on the fate of nations, especially if they offer populist remedies for current ills.

But if integrity is not lodged in contemporary politics, the same cannot be said for life outside the intrigues and grandstanding of a leader's entourage. A Google search for 'integrity loss' as I write this gave me 429 million results in less than a third of a second.[18] The first two pages of its printout alone fairly represented the vast variety of contexts in which integrity occurs, including a person's character, structural failure causing injury, data completeness, marine losses, wellbore casing, recruitment agency deception and the corporate sector.

It all seems a far cry from the moment at the beginning of this book where we found the word's origin in the Latin *integritas*! But there is the word, and the meaning that goes with it. In this case, as I stressed, the bridging of completeness and principles that the concept of integrity carried with it from its earliest beginning is precisely the source of its everlasting adaptability and extension over multiple contexts that have characterized all subsequent uses of the word. This was a moment of conceptual innovation with an intuition of what is distinctive about human existence, the growth of culture, well before it was recognized in the eighteenth century. The genealogy of the term marks key developmental moments in western history and tracks the expansion of the West to the present where its legacy has been assimilated into a world society.[19] It is part of what I called earlier the West's unwinding, the worldwide acquisition of its products, material and cultural, including among them the English language.

The conflicts that pervade public and private life echo to the sound of appeals for integrity or accusations of its loss. In both cases, attention is focused on desired standards of behaviour, on threats to our environment or to the dangers of new technologies. But these can never obliterate the impetus that the quest for integrity has given to the changes in contemporary society that have benefited millions of people worldwide.

The balance sheet of the costs and benefits of the headlong processes of change in society today is never finalized. Indeed, the quest for integrity chases ever-receding goals. There can be no end to a search for equality, or for self-realization, or for justice, and yet, for each, a check for integrity along the way provides a reflexive assessment of travel towards a destination along a long and winding road. Yet it is a pilgrim's progress in a secular world. Having been a driver of western development in the past along with all those factors, the quest for integrity has now become the property of worldwide human society. In that context, there is an open possibility that its benefits can become a positive contribution to a world where traditional values are under so much threat.

This book has aimed to show that the West's drive for integrity has foregrounded things rather than relationships. In the context of other cultures worldwide, it has been the exception. The predominant vision of reality elsewhere is of a world where the relations of human beings with each other and with nature constitute an immanent reality.

There is a poetic truth behind the emergence of the idea of the World Wide Web of internet technology. It replicates the sense of traditional human relations before modernity. It represents the potential convergence of integrity-driven innovation with age-old wisdom for human survival on this Earth. The West and the rest of the world come together, and it is people everywhere who can imagine and work for a better future.

The internet is a fine example of the fruits of scientific integrity, advancing technology for the benefit of human communication. Not all directions of scientific research have the same benign outcomes. The risks entailed in the advance of generative artificial intelligence are unlimited. Plagiarism in student essays is at the trivial extreme (but serious for the pupil–teacher relationship); the ultimate outcome could be extinction of our species by autonomous weapons systems.

For the benefit of the human race, integrity needs to relinquish the exclusive embrace of sovereign entities and extend its concern towards relations between them. We have examined the lack of institutional integrity in so many corporate scandals resulting from the tunnel vision of operatives each pursuing narrowly defined tasks, neglecting the overall set of relations that make up the integrity of an organization. Institutional integrity lodged in codes is one way of redressing that imbalance. Even more important is the professional outlook that extends beyond the immediate task to the organization as a whole and, beyond that, to the wider society.[20]

Overwhelmingly in our time, the most important sector for observing the demands of integrity is that of relations between people. It applies at every level, where Presidents Biden and Xi meet, between their advisers too, among themselves and across the political and cultural divides. That sharing in common humanity applies equally in rescuing migrants in the English Channel or assisting them at the Mexican border. It is foundational for interpersonal relations.[21]

To aid our awareness of the present imperative, I want to recall a book lost in another time of chaos, between the two world wars, *Imperialism and Civilization* (1928), which made an appeal to 'what we now call western or European civilization'.[22] It asked for a declaration of an end to imperialism and, to support its antithesis, the League of Nations, 'an international society of interrelated rather than warring parts'.[23] The author, Leonard Woolf, called for a synthesis of civilizations. Today, we are more inclined to think in terms of nations within one world civilization, but his message was effectively the same as in this book.

Yet we know what happened a little more than a decade after that book was published. And the signs today are the same as then – that calls for tolerance, respect, cooperation and rejection of violence will go unheeded as nations rush to rearm. We must hope that the technologies of communication will be the transformative difference from that earlier time, and we must work for that integrity in human relationships which can make a corresponding contribution to securing peace for our children and for generations to come.

Notes

Preface

1 It used to be at the centre of the motto on the coat of arms at Donald Trump's estate at Mar-a-Lago. (He replaced it with '*Trump*'.) Jemima Kelly. 'Dispatch from Mar-a-Lago', *FT Weekend Magazine*, 26–7 November 2022, p. 18. In a subsequent report, 'The In Crowd', also in *FT Weekend Magazine*, 2–3 March 2024, p. 18, Kelly tells how the coat of arms now decorates everything from the gates to the shampoo bottles in the showers.

2 *Financial Times*, Javier Espinosa, 'EU to Fine Big Tech over Poll Disinformation', 21 March 2024, p. 8; ibid., Alistair Gray and Daniel Thomas, 'News Corp Claimants Seek Murdoch in Court', p. 3.

3 ASRC News, Photonics Initiative, 'Scientists Achieve Major Breakthrough in Preserving Integrity of Sound Waves', 17 July 2020. https://asrc.gc.cuny.edu/topics/photonics-initiative/ Although 'integrity' appears in the title, it does not actually get mentioned in the main body of the report.

Chapter 1 An Ancient Legacy for the West

1 Oswald Spengler (1926 [1920/22]), *The Decline of the West* [*Der Untergang des Abendlandes*].

2 As in R. J. Hollingdale's translation of Friedrich Nietzsche's *Götzendämmerung* (1889) (*Twilight of the Idols and the Antichrist* [1968]), see pp. 25, 77, 96, etc. This does not prevent Charles Taylor in his monumental study *Hegel* (1975) from inferring that the German philosopher was in fact writing about what in English would be called integrity when 'external reality [which] embodies us and on which we depend is fully expressive of us and contains nothing alien', p. 148. This completeness is only obtained by people seeing themselves as emanations of universal *Geist* (spirit). I think Taylor is fully justified in his inference. In fact, Hegel is giving added emphasis to the meaning of integrity, without finding an equivalent term in German but only via roundabout phrases like 'consciousness first finds in self-consciousness – the notion of mind – its turning point, where it leaves the part-coloured show of the sensuous immediate, passes from the dark void of the transcendent and remote super-sensuous, and steps into the spiritual daylight of the present' (G. W. F. Hegel, *The Phenomenology of Mind* [1931 (1807)], trans. J. B. Baillie). 'Integrity' is more succinct!

3 I am greatly indebted to the late Reverend Dr D. H. Matthews, a native Welsh speaker, for informing me on these points.

4 I am very grateful to Dr Frances Yiying Zhang of the Confucius Institute, Goldsmiths, University of London, for providing the Chinese characters and translations.

5 Fritjof Capra (1976), *The Tao of Physics*, p. 121.

6 Joseph Needham (1969), *The Grand Titration: Science and Society in East and West*, p. 234.

7 Bertrand Russell (1945), *A History of Western Philosophy*, p. 66.

8 Iain McGilchrist, psychiatrist and literary scholar, has highlighted these differences in his extensive study of the respective contributions that the left and right hemispheres of the brain make to human behaviour, and points to the dominance of the left, analytical side of the brain in westerners and the more balanced use of both sides in East Asians. He leaves open the etiology of the difference, whether it is cultural in origin or physiological

(*The Master and his Emissary: The Divided Brain and the Making of the Western World*, 2009, p. 458).

9 Lucretius (1982), *On the Nature of Things*, trans. W. H. D. Rouse, revised by Martin F. Smith.

10 Lucretius would have had no difficulty in understanding the symmetry between the modern knowledge of nature, for example of molecules, with his account of human integrity. Thus the molecule for DNA is held together by van der Waal forces of hydrogen bonds. 'The forces involved in these links are just enough to hold the bonds together and maintain the integrity of the molecule' (Charles Cockell, *The Equations of Life*, 2019, p. 7). They are vital for the reproduction of biological cells. The integrity of that molecule thus provides for the possibility of reproductive life. Lucretius used *integer* and its derivatives as a common reference as in the virgin spring (*On the Nature of Things* I, 927, IV, 2); of food as a renewal (II, 1146); asserting the wholeness of spirit and mind (III, 705); of the unbroken vessel for wine (VI, 231); for lightning strikes that leave objects unbroken (VI, 348).

11 The *Oxford Latin Dictionary* (1982) provides three basic meanings of *integritas*:

1. Soundness, wholeness (of the body or mind)
2. The quality of being unadulterated, purity (esp. of style)
3. a. Moral uprightness, probity, integrity; b. (esp. of women) chastity

It offers citations for each of these meanings from a contemporary of Lucretius, Cicero (106–43 BC), whose book *Brutus* was a history of Rome as viewed through past speech making. I am grateful to Mary Beard for her advice on my sources. She bears no responsibility for the conclusions I draw.

12 Margaret E. Mohrmann (2004), 'Integrity: Integritas, Innocentia, Simplicitas', *Journal of the Society of Christian Ethics* 24: 25–37.

13 Ibid., p. 29.

14 Ibid., p. 35. Such a state was achieved by extreme self-denial, as with the anchoress, walled up in a cell and seeing visions. An example was Julian (St Juliana) of Norwich (1342–1416?). Clifton Wolters, introducing Julian's *Revelations of Divine Love* (1966, p. 29), raises the question of the 'integrity of her visions' which she experienced in 1373, a question that exposes the furthest reaches of the all-embracing idea of integrity as it extends into non-material realms, scope that it owes to the early Christian lodging of values in another reality. For human beings, integrity implies the bonding of the material and the spiritual.

15 Aquinas, *Selected Political Writings* (1954), ed. A. P. D'Entreves, trans. J. G. Dawson, p. 81.

16 *Oxford English Dictionary, Compact Edition* (1971), Vol. 1, p. 1455. [Vol. I. of the 12-volume edn of 1933, p. 368.]

17 The same reference is cited in the *Middle English Dictionary*, op. cit., p. 235.

18 *Oxford English Dictionary: Compact Edition*, op. cit. First reference 1548 for qualities attributed to English King Henry VI.

19 Middle English took it over from the French more or less at the same time as 'integrite'. Around 1460, a register of Oseney Abbey near Oxford recorded a gift from the lord of the manor as follows: 'We graunte the church of seynte George . . . with all his integrite or holnesse and with all his pertinencies and particles . . .', in Sherman M. Kuhn and John Reedy (eds), *Middle English Dictionary* (1968).

20 Mohrmann, op. cit., p. 35.

21 Ibid.

22 Just as a foretaste of the limbo that integrity now inhabits in our own time, consider the poem entitled 'Marriages' by Philip Larkin, written in 1951. Given his own resistance to marriage, its 'integrity of self-hatred' could well be Larkin's own chosen persona, about as far from the integrity of an Ambrose as could be imagined! *Collected Poems*, 1988, p. 63.

23 Fernand Braudel (1995 [1963]), *A History of Civilizations*, p. 23.

24 Ibid., p. 333.

25 In a brilliant tract written between the two world wars, Leonard Woolf (1928) also adopted a long view of western history, announcing the end of imperialism and the need to bring civilizations together. His hopes were dashed. Is integrity the missing link from his account that might have prevented the looming disaster? That thought encourages me to write this book.

Chapter 2 Integrity Becomes Modern

1 Stephen Greenblatt writes of the 'key role played by Lucretius in early modern philosophy'. *The Swerve* (2012), p. 296.
2 Ibid., p. 244.
3 *Grand Larousse de la Langue Française* (1975), Paris: Librairie Larousse, Vol. 4, p. 2742.
4 Greenblatt, op. cit., p. 234.
5 Niccolo Machiavelli (1903 [1532]), *The Prince*, ch. 18, p. 69. Machiavelli probably spent much of the year 1513 writing his book. It circulated widely before his death but was only officially published with the approval of Pope Clement VII in 1532 before being put on the Catholic Index of forbidden books in 1559. It had already been translated into French, and editions in Latin, English and German followed.
6 Ibid., p. 71.
7 Ibid.
8 Ibid., p. 105.
9 Bertrand Russell (1938), *Power: A New Social Analysis*, p. 35.
10 Ibid., p. 97.
11 Lord Acton (1891), 'Introduction' to Niccolo Machiavelli, *Il Principe*, ed. L. Arthur Bird, pp. xix-xx.
12 Ibid., p. xl.
13 Ibid., p. 243. Quoting from Shakespeare's *Romeo and Juliet*, Act I, Scene IV, line 58.
14 The quotations from Shakespeare's plays that follow are derived from a list obtained on 12/08/2003 from www://languid.org/cgibin/shakespeare?st=search&keywords=integrity&operation, as follows:

The Two Gentlemen of Verona: Act III, scene II, line 77.

Love's Labour's Lost: Act V, scene II, line 357.

Measure for Measure: Act IV, scene II, line 204; Act V, scene I, line 108.

Coriolanus: Act III, Scene I, line 158.

Cymbeline: Act V, scene V, line 44.

Henry VIII: Act II, scene IV, line 57; Act III, scene I, lines 7 and 50; Act III, scene II, line 454; Act V, scene I, line 115; Act V, scene III, line 145.

15 Francis Bacon (2002 [1625]), 'The Essays or Counsels Civil and Moral', *The Major Works*, edited by Brian Vickers, p. 379.

16 Ibid., p. 446.

17 Lisa Jardine and Alan Stewart (1999), *Hostage to Fortune: the Troubled Life of Francis Bacon 1561–1626*, p. 503.

18 See Francis Bacon (2002 [1605]), op. cit., pp. 120–299.

19 Ibid., pp. 457–90.

20 In an excerpt from *The Advancement of Learning*, in Arthur Johnston (ed.) (1965), *Francis Bacon*, p. 33.

21 Machiavelli, op. cit., p. 69.

22 Bernard Mandeville (1989 [1724]), *The Fable of the Bees*, ed. P. Harth.

23 Ibid., p. 348.

24 *Bolingbroke on the Spirit of Patriotism and on the Idea of a Patriot King* (1926 [1749]), ed. A. Hassall.

25 Ibid., p. 111.

26 Samuel Johnson (1785), *A Dictionary of the English Language*, 6th edn, Vol. 1.

27 Samuel Johnson (1975 [1759]), *Rasselas*, p. 144. The poignancy of this advice is made all the greater by Johnson depicting him as mad, deluded into thinking that his knowledge gave him control of the weather and the movement of the sun.

28 Boswell noted how he kept a record in Latin of his illnesses until near his death on 13 December 1784. Ibid., p. 584.

29 *The Works of Samuel Johnson* (1825), 9 vols, vol. 1, pp. 386–9.

30 James Boswell (1906 [1791]), *The Life of Dr Johnson*, vol. 2, p. 597.

Chapter 3 The American Experience

1 Adam Smith (1868 [1776]), *An Inquiry into the Nature and Causes of the Wealth of Nations*, p. 258. The second such event was the discovery of the passage to the East Indies via the Cape of Good Hope. This of course opened up economic opportunities at the time that even surpassed those in the western hemisphere.

2 Weber's study of *The Protestant Ethic and the Spirit of Capitalism* was first published as journal articles in 1904–5, and later in the first volume of his collected essays on the sociology of religion (Weber 2009 [1920]). He pointed to the importance of financial success for the Protestant believers as a sign of the individual's standing in the eyes of God, and therefore of eventual salvation. As an additional factor in stimulating economic activity, we should also add the importance of a direct relation with the creator God, the One who had made all things. This the Protestant gained in escaping the intermediation of the Catholic priest. Innovation as well as financial gain spurred early capitalist development.

3 Max Weber (2009 [1920]), trans. Stephen Kalberg, *The Protestant Ethic and the Spirit of Capitalism with Other Writings on the Rise of the West*, p. 70.

4 Weber, ibid., pp. 72–3.

5 *Benjamin Franklin's Autobiography* (1986 [1793]), ed. A. Leo Lemay and P. M. Zall, pp. 351–2.

6 Ibid., p. 46.

7 Ibid., pp. 67–8.

8 Ibid., p. 75.

9 Ibid., p. 76.

10 Ibid.

11 Ibid., pp. 67–8.

12 William J. Bennett (1997), *The Spirit of America*, p. 162.

13 Ibid., p. 236.

14 Ibid., p. 151. Note, integrity is a quality of mind, as such not a virtue.
15 Ibid., p. 313.
16 Ibid., p. 243.
17 W. E. Channing (1870), *The Complete Works*, p. 272. Channing's nephew, a poet of the same name, was the closest friend of Nathaniel Hawthorne, who famously depicted the stringencies of Puritanism in his novel *The Scarlet Letter* (1850). In a preface to it, he describes another close friend working with him at the time in the Custom House in Salem: 'His integrity was perfect; it was a law of nature with him, rather than a choice or a principle.' In this way, Hawthorne points to the ultimate fusion of nature and morality which the ever-receding goal of integrity promises and that the normal mortal can never attain. (Hawthorne, 2000 [1850], p. 2).
18 Marianne Weber (1974 [1926]), *Max Weber: A Biography*, trans. Harry Zohn, p. 86.
19 Alexis de Tocqueville (1994 [1835–40]), *Democracy in America*, ed. J. P. Mayer, pp. 547–9.
20 Ibid., p. 150.
21 William G. Sumner (1919), 'Integrity in Education', in *The Forgotten Man and Other Essays*, Vol. 4, pp. 409–19. The editor A. G. Keller writes that it was probably delivered in the 1880s.
22 Ibid., p. 409.
23 Ibid., p. 410.
24 Ibid., pp. 413–14.
25 Hugo Munsterberg (1904), *The Americans*, p. 600.
26 James MacGregor and Susan Dunn (2001), *The Three Roosevelts: Patrician Leaders who Transformed America*, pp. 22–4. Its use revived by the author J. K. Rowling for the headmaster of Hogwarts, the word has been given recent currency in British politics when Boris Johnson referred in a column in the *Sun* newspaper to Labour leader Jeremy Corbyn as a 'mutton-headed old mugwump'. Though condescending, to say the least, it could

even be seen as mildly affectionate (apart from 'mutton-headed', of course)'.

27 Ibid., pp. 29, 35.

28 *Wikipedia*, 'Grover Cleveland', updated 23 October 2020. It was a personal ticket that lost value when it was revealed Cleveland had fathered an illegitimate son, another illustration of the dangers of self-proclaimed integrity, though Cleveland just scraped through to become the 22nd president of the United States.

29 Quoted by Kwasi Kwarteng (2011), *Ghosts of Empire: Britain's Legacies in the Modern World*, p. 292, from an article 'Education in Tropical Africa' by Lugard in the *Edinburgh Review* (July 1925): 2–9.

30 Sumner, op. cit., p. 405. 'The Science of Sociology', speech delivered on 9 November, 1882.

31 Quoted by J. D. Y. Peel (1971), *Herbert Spencer: The Evolution of a Sociologist*, p. 101.

32 Herbert Spencer (1910 [1862]), *First Principles*, Vol. 2, p. 291.

33 Sociology became the new gospel for that time in the United States. Sumner himself had once been a Protestant minister.

34 Quoted by J. D. Y. Peel, op. cit., p. 2.

35 Robin M. Williams Jr (1966), *American Society: A Sociological Interpretation*.

36 Ibid., pp. 5–6.

37 The chapter begins by citing a previous book by Robert C. Angell (1941), *The Integration of American Society*, ibid., p. 541.

38 Ibid., p. 544.

39 Ibid., p. 545.

40 A British sociologist, David Lockwood, made a similar distinction between system integration and social integration, where the former refers to power and economic relations while the latter is based on shared experience and values. (See 'Social Integration and System Integration', in Z. Zollschan and W. Hirsch (eds) (1964), *Explorations in Social Change*, pp. 244–56.)

41 Talcott Parsons (1951), *The Social System*.

42 Talcott Parsons (1954), *Essays in Sociological Theory*, pp. 412–13.

43 Talcott Parsons (1953), 'The Theory of Symbolism in Relation to Action', in Parsons, Robert F. Bales and Edward A. Shils (eds), *Working Papers in the Theory of Action*, p. 53.

44 Talcott Parsons and Edward A. Shils (eds) (1962), *Toward a General Theory of Action*, p. 26.

45 Talcott Parsons (1954), op. cit., p. 399.

46 Talcott Parsons and E. A. Shils (eds) (1962), op. cit., p. 26.

47 Talcott Parsons (1954), op. cit., p. 143.

48 Stephen Kalberg (2014), *Searching for the Spirit of American Democracy: Max Weber's Analysis of a Unique Political Culture, Past, Present, and Future*, p. 1.

Chapter 4 The Elusiveness of Personal Integrity

1 *Benjamin Franklin's Autobiography* (1986 [1793]), ed. J. A. Leo Lemay and P. M. Zall, pp. 259–66. Poe's story was originally published in the *Broadway Journal*, 2 August 1845, pp. 49–52.

2 Ibid., p. 262.

3 Ibid., pp. 67–8.

4 Ibid., p. 290.

5 Ibid., p. 296.

6 Ibid., p. 295.

7 Ibid., Lawrence's essay 'Benjamin Franklin' was published originally in his *Studies in Classic American Literature* (1923), pp. 13–31. Lemay and Zall (op. cit., p. 365) point out that he accused Franklin (and America) of lacking spirituality.

8 Maurice Merleau-Ponty (1973), *The Prose of the World*, p. 133.

9 Melanie Klein (1975), *The Collected Writings*, 4 vols. An example of how that programme could inform popular culture and how it melded with integrity can be found in Nena O'Neill and George O'Neill (1973), *Open Marriage: A New Life Style for Couples*, p. 209: 'Having identity means that you know who you are. You are able to be an authentic person in your disclosures to others. You have integrity.'

10 Arthur Koestler (1970), *The Ghost in the Machine*. In his open hierarchical systems, 'holons' refer to any sub-holon in a rule-governed system. It asserts its individuality but functions as part of a larger integrated whole. See pp. 253, 383.

11 Jeremy Griffith (1988), *Free: The End of the Human Condition*, pp. 29–31.

12 Erich Fromm (1956), *The Sane Society*, p. 31.

13 Erich Fromm (1942), *The Fear of Freedom*, pp. 225–7.

14 Ibid., p. 231.

15 Ibid., p. 247.

16 Ibid., I should make it clear that this is my own conviction too.

17 Erich Fromm (1957), *The Art of Loving*, p. 48.

18 Fromm (1942), p. 118.

19 Tom Driberg (1978), *Ruling Passions*. We will look more closely at Driberg's claim to integrity later in this chapter.

20 When he asked Virginia Woolf how he could improve a novel that her publishing firm, The Hogarth Press, had just rejected, after lengthy discussion, she told him to scrap it. She was, he wrote humbly, 'a most scrupulous artist who demanded high standards of artistic integrity from others'. Spender (1951), *World within World*, p. 157.

21 Stephen Spender (1969), *The Year of the Young Rebels*, p. 115.

22 Ibid., pp. 133–5.

23 Paul Goodman (1960), *Growing up Absurd*, p. 172.

24 Ibid., p. 28.

25 'It is necessary to preserve one's personal integrity if only to influence the future when the emergency is past.' Ibid., p. 68.

26 Ibid., p.189

27 Ibid., p. 280.

28 Ibid., p. 283.

29 Ibid., p. 13.

30 Ibid., p. 91.

31 William H. Whyte (1956), *The Organization Man*.

32 Goodman, op. cit., p. 91.

33 See below, note 48.

34 To be fair to the heated climate of debate among sociologists at the time, we should recall the trenchant attack on the interactionist paradigm in the famous paper by Dennis Wrong, 'The Over-Socialized Conception of Man in Modern Sociology', *American Sociological Review* 26 (1961): 183–93.

35 Goodman, op. cit., back cover extract from Webster Schott in *The Nation*.

36 Spender (1969), op. cit., p. 51.

37 Spender (1951), *World within World*, p. 254.

38 Ibid., p. 255.

39 Matthew Spender (2015), *A House in St John's Wood: In Search of My Parents*, p. 44.

40 Ibid.

41 Quoted by Francis Wheen (1990), *Tom Driberg: His Life and Indiscretions*, p. 414.

42 Tom Driberg (1978), op. cit.

43 Ibid., p. 143.

44 Wheen, op. cit., p. 409.

45 Ibid., p. 394.

46 Ibid., p. 419.

47 Ibid., p. 420.

48 George H. Mead (1934), *Mind, Self and Society*, 3 vols, 'The social or impersonal aspect of the self integrates it with the social group to which it belongs' (Vol. 1, p. 321).

49 Erving Goffman (1967), *Interaction Ritual: Essays on Face-to-Face Behavior*, pp. 44–5.

50 Erving Goffman (1971), *The Presentation of Self in Everyday Life*. The Edinburgh professor of sociology, Tom Burns, noted that the book had sold over half a million copies before 1980 and that reviewers of his last book, *Forms of Talk* (1981), who included Christopher Ricks, then professor of English in Cambridge, and the playwright Alan Bennett, were lavish in praising it for 'grace', 'wit', 'untiring perspicacity', 'humour and imagination' (Burns, 1992, *Erving Goffman*, p. 1.)

51 Erving Goffman (1968), *Stigma: Notes on the Management of Spoiled Identity*, p. 153.

52 Erving Goffman (1968), *Asylums: Essays on the Social Situation of Mental Patients and Other Inmates*, p. 30.

53 Erving Goffman (1971), op. cit., p. 21.

54 Ibid., p. 83.

55 Ibid., p. 75.

56 Erving Goffman (1975), *Frame Analysis: An Essay on the Organization of Experience*, pp. 574–5.

57 Erving Goffman (1971), op. cit., p. 247.

58 Erving Goffman (1975), *Frame Analysis*, p. 572.

59 Ibid., p. 573.

60 Ibid.

61 Ibid., p. 575, quoting from Maurice Merleau-Ponty; see above, note 8.

62 Erving Goffman (1971), *Relations in Public: Microstudies of the Public Order*.

63 Paul Halmos (1970), *The Personal Service Society*, pp. 166–8.

64 Anthony Giddens (1991), *Modernity and Self-Identity: Self and Society in the Late Modern Age*, p. 80.

65 Anthony Giddens (1992), *The Transformation of Intimacy: Sexuality, Love and Eroticism in Modern Societies*, p. 191.

Chapter 5 Creative Integrity

1 The Nobel Prize in Literature 1964 – Press Release. The remarks at the banquet were made by S. Friberg, Rector of the Caroline Institute.   http://www.nobelprize.org/nobel_prizes/literature/laureates/1964/press.html

2 Rebecca Solint (2021), *Orwell's Roses*, p. 229. She reflects on what integrity meant for Orwell: 'That integrity, those honoured contracts, those endeavors to reach out and make whole through the use of words that connect, empower, liberate, illuminate are the beauty to which he is most committed and the one he most celebrates, in the writing of others and in his own efforts as

a writer.' (It is a rare example of a book that actually indexes integrity.)

3 Hanif Kureishi, 'I do not know whether it will do . . .' *Guardian*, 28 May 2016, p. 5.

4 Stephen Spender (1951), *World within World*, p. 157. See also above, ch. 4, note 20.

5 Ibid., p. 159.

6 Noel Annan (1990), *Our Age: Portrait of a Generation*, p. 87.

7 Vita Sackville-West (1930), *The Edwardians*, pp. 19–20.

8 Marx was not invariably so absolute on art and alienation. In his notebooks written in 1857–8, he allowed for the contemporary appreciation of Greek mythology: 'A man cannot become a child again, or he becomes childish. But does he not find joy in the child's naïveté, and must he not strive to reproduce its truth at a higher stage?' (*Grundrisse*, 1973, p. 111).

9 Frances Partridge (1981), *Memories*, p. 76.

10 Clive Bell (1988 [1956]), *Old Friends*, p. 130.

11 Ibid., p. 137.

12 Clive Bell (1928), *Civilization: An Essay*, p. v.

13 Ibid., p. 59.

14 Ibid., p. 117.

15 Ibid., p. 164.

16 Ibid., p. 167.

17 Ibid., p. 192.

18 She died from drowning herself, 28 March 1941.

19 Daniel Bell (1980), *The Winding Passage: Essays and Sociological Journeys 1960–1980*, p. 130.

20 'The "Intelligentsia" in American Society', in ibid., pp. 119–37. This was a lecture originally given at the Hebrew Union College in Cincinnati in 1976.

21 The lecture questioning the nature of social entities' existence concluded with a possible dig at his Harvard colleague, Talcott Parsons. The founders of the United States, Bell wrote, 'made . . . a political revolution in the demand for liberty; yet it was a revolution within a transcendental frame, and that frame gave it

vision and drive.' So much for integration around values! Ibid., pp. 136–7. Of course, as we have seen, there were many radical voices who opposed Parsons's integrative vision, but Bell worked from a quite different set of assumptions.

22 Dorian Lynskey (no title), *Guardian G2*, p. 5. 13 March 2012.

23 Jennifer Williams, n.d., *Common Threads for Uncommon People*, p. 27.

24 Charles Madge (1964), *Society in the Mind: Elements of Social Eidos*, p. 146.

25 Ibid., p. 138.

26 William Wordsworth (1971), *The Prelude*, ed. J. C. Maxwell, p. 18.

27 Ibid., p. 54.

28 Ibid.

29 This is, of course, just one direction into which one can take the idea of spirit. It has been interpreted in many different ways, historically and across cultures. When the mystery of life in the human body was attributed to the soul by the Vitalists of the eighteenth century, it was something that inhabited it and left at the time of death. But that raised a further issue in the controversy between materialism and idealism. 'Spirit, however refined, must still be material,' said a radical thinker of the time, John Thelwall. (Quoted in Richard Holmes, 2008, *The Age of Wonder: How the Romantic Generation Discovered the Beauty and Terror of Science*, p. 316.)

30 An acute anthropologist aimed to correct that prejudice when he wrote of the 'man of action' in primitive cultures. He was absorbed in 'attempting to coerce the object' precisely because its reality is not all that we see at any one time (Paul Radin, 1957, *Primitive Man as Philosopher*, p. 246). He comprehensively rebutted the idea of some kind of prelogical mentality among pre-literate peoples.

31 J. J. M. de Groot (1918), *Universismus: Die Grundlage der Religion und Ethik, des Staatswesens und der Wissenschaften Chinas*.

32 See Wang Yiwei (2016), *The Belt and Road Initiative: What will China Offer to the World in Its Rise*, p. 189, Appendix: 'Vision and Proposed Actions Outlined on Jointly Building Silk Road Economic Belt and 21st-Century Maritime Silk Road', full text of the action plan authorized by the State Council in 2015.

33 For an examination of the way the ancient concept has been assimilated into contemporary Chinese political discourse, see Martin Albrow and JIN Wei, 'Spirit (精神 *jing shen*) as a Key Contemporary Chinese Concept', in *Journal of China in Global and Comparative Perspective* 7 (2021). Republished in Martin Albrow, ed. Xiangqun Chang (2021), *China and the Shared Human Future: Exploring Common Values and Goals*, pp. 378–92. The same book includes a comment by its editor and the author's brief reflection on integrity in cultural perspective on pp. 397–400.

34 Xi Jinping (2014), *The Governance of China*, p. 33.

35 Ibid., p. 52.

36 My thanks to Frances Yiying Zhang for providing the Chinese language terms.

37 Even Wordsworth was not immune, though he referred often to spirit and soul. Rachel Hewitt (*A Revolution of Feeling*, 2017, p. 427) gives as an example of the influence of secularization how he replaced 'soul' with 'mind' in one place in the last version of *The Prelude*.

38 Gilbert Ryle provides a casual example of this banal use of spirit when he offers to illustrate a category mistake when a foreigner asks where team spirit in cricket is to be found. It is not, says Ryle, a third thing beyond bowling or catching. He says it is 'roughly, the keenness with which each of the special tasks is performed' (*The Concept of Mind*, 1949, p. 17). We may note he is not inclined to suggest it is the property of the team as a whole. British individualism will not allow it.

39 Edward W. Said (1994), *Culture and Imperialism*.

40 Jane Austen (1980 [1814]), *Mansfield Park*, pp. 59, 333.

41 Ibid., p. 266.

42 Said, op. cit., p. 116.

43 Ibid., p. 408.

44 Ibid., p. xxix.

45 See chapter 6 for the debates that surrounded the design for the memorial.

46 For his founding inspiration, see Graham Leicester (2016), *Transformative Innovation.*

47 For his proposals to coordinate integrity with systems thinking for solutions to world problems today, see Anthony Hodgson (2019), *Systems Thinking for a Turbulent World: A Search for New Perspectives.*

48 My paper originally prepared for the group, 'Local Integrities and Global Interconnectedness', was published in Martin Albrow, 2014, *Global Age Essays on Social and Cultural Change,* pp. 127–37.

49 Only recently (29 November 2023), there has been a vivid reminder that nothing in the world stays still. The *Falkirk Herald* reports in its Business section, 'Jobs under threat as union enters discussion with management at Grangemouth rubber plan . . . closure of the site in now on the table for discussion.'

Chapter 6 Being Human

1 Lucretius, trans. W. H. D. Rouse, rev. M. F. Smith (1982), *On the Nature of Things (De Rerum Natura),* p. 35.

2 Paul Radin (1957 [1927]), *Primitive Man as Philosopher,* p. 320.

3 Mircea Eliade (1954), *The Myth of the Eternal Return,* pp. 81–4.

4 Ibid., p. 76.

5 Ibid., p. 80.

6 Jean-Paul Sartre (1988 [1953]), *Being and Nothingness: An Essay on Phenomenological Ontology.*

7 Ibid., p. 624.

8 Ibid., p. xvii.

9 John Rawls (1999 [1971]), *Theory of Justice,* pp. 455–6. Bernard Williams discusses authenticity in relation to sincerity in his *Truth and Truthfulness: An Essay in Genealogy* (2002). It was

an issue that arose, he writes, first in the eighteenth century. We can say that it is a development beyond older understandings of integrity and related to the distinction between self and self-understanding, each of which gave rise to different schools of thought, the latter in the sociology of *Verstehen* (understanding) in Germany and the former in the symbolic interactionism of Chicago and Erving Goffman. We may recall that Goffman attributed integrity to the performance, rather than the person. Williams points out that the quest for authenticity can lead to ethical and social disaster (p. 205). We can say the same for the pursuit of integrity. (I am grateful to Greville Healey for referring me to Williams's book).

10 Ibid., p. xvi.

11 Dworkin (1985), *A Matter of Principle*, p. 107.

12 *The Collected Works of Ancient Chinese Philosophy: Lao Zi Says* (2013 [5th century]), p. 37.

13 I am grateful to Frances Yiying Zhang of the Confucius Institute, Goldsmiths, University of London, for providing the Chinese characters and translations.

14 Confucius, trans. D. C. Lau (1979), *The Analects*, p. 125.

15 Feng Youlan (1939), *Xin yuan ren* [A New Treatise on the Nature of Man]. For the references and interpretation of the Chinese idea of the complete person, I am greatly indebted to Dr Zhang Xiaoying, Professor at the Beijing Foreign Studies University and Director of the Confucius Institute in Tirana University, Albania.

16 Alasdair MacIntyre (1985), *After Virtue*, p, 203.

17 In political sociology, following Max Weber, the term 'charisma' is applied to persons who attract followers. This has given rise to arguments about whether the exceptional qualities belong to the person or exist in the minds of disciples or party members. It has to be both: they are inseparable.

18 I was in the United States at the time, a Fellow in the Woodrow Wilson Center, situated plumb between the White House and Capitol Hill. The impeachment of the president was the coffee-break conversation filler. But globalization was the crowd puller.

When Thomas L. Friedman, author of *The Lexus and the Olive Tree* (1999), celebrating the new global reach of American power, arrived to give a speech in the Center, the audience rose to give him a standing welcome. The message was so powerful at the time.

19 Humberto R. Maturana and Francisco J. Varela (1981), *Autopoiesis and Cognition: The Realization of the Living*. In the recent past, cybernetics has developed mechanical feedback concepts, while Maturana and Varela have developed systems theory for biological sciences, coining the term 'Autopoiesis' to mean self-regeneration.

20 The engagement with Marxist ideas in western thought has been a stimulus to creative thinking and, in effect, challenges to find new intellectual beginnings. For instance, the disillusioned believer in Marxism, Arthur Koestler, sought a resolution of the integrity/integration dilemma by creating a hierarchy of interdependent social entities that he called holons, right up to humanity at the top of the pyramid. See chapter 4, note 10.

21 James Lovelock (1988), *The Age of Gaia*; Lynn Margulis (1993), *Symbiosis in Cell Evolution.*

22 In one of his contributions to the *Neue Rheische Zeitung* (No. 266, 7 April 1849), Marx writes, 'A Negro is a Negro. He only becomes a slave in certain relations. In production men enter into relation not only with nature.' This last remark was amended in the 1891 edition (in other words, after his death in 1883) to read 'not only act on nature but also on one another'. (Karl Marx and Frederick Engels, 1977, *Collected Works*, Vol. 9, p. 211). With these subtle changes, there is a library of distinctions to be made. Marx's social relations of production here are precisely ones that are entered into as a person. Relations with nature, e.g., with animals, eating, breathing, and reproduction are excluded in the amended version but could be implied in the first formulation. This is emphasized further on where Marx writes 'only within these social connections and relations does their relation with nature, does production, take place', which the 1891 edition also

amends to 'action on nature' instead of 'relation with nature'. That 'a Negro is a Negro' only in certain social definitions of natural relations seems to drop out of possible consideration. Hannah Arendt's scope of consideration of relations is emphatically broader, as is the Daoist.

23 Hannah Arendt (1998 [1958]), *The Human Condition*, p. 234. Arendt was writing before 'men' was a proscribed term. We would write 'human beings' or just 'humans' today.

24 Ibid., p. 238.

25 Ibid., p. 233.

26 Ibid., p. 183.

27 Stephen L. Carter, *Integrity*, 1996, p. 226.

28 Ibid., p. 241.

Chapter 7 Media Storms in the New Century

1 The need for such a reference to the time and the state of the world is still there. For the reading public, writers often resort to the use of 'zeitgeist' to get round the mawkish impression of 'spirit of the age'. And German always sounds more intelligent.

2 The seminal text for American corporate global strategies of the 1980s was Theodore Levitt's 1983 article 'The Globalization of Markets', *Harvard Business Review*, May–June, pp. 92–102.

3 'Remarks by the President at America's Millennium Gala', 31 December 1999. National Archives and Records Administration. https://clintonwhitehouse4.archives.gov/WH/New/html/20000104.html

4 For insider accounts of the impact of the affair on public perceptions, see Clinton's speech writer, Michael Waldman (2000), *Potus Speaks*, pp. 201–61, and his senior adviser, Sidney Blumenthal (2003), *The Clinton Wars*, pp. 325–696.

5 Al Gore (1992), *Earth in the Balance*, p. 176.

6 This standard expectation was forthrightly affirmed in the second edition of a celebrated text for the time, Robert Pirsig's *Zen and the Art of Motorcycle Maintenance* (1999). Printed in an appendix there is an email exchange where Pirsig is asked about

a statement (p. 341) by the book's narrator that 'we do need a return to individual integrity, self-reliance and old fashioned gumption'. He responds, 'I don't know of any political reaction that opposes [them]. Both Republicans and Democrats seem to claim that is their position . . . the narrator is coming up with a cliché here . . .' (p. 411).

7 Kevin Phillips (2004), *American Dynasty*, p. 39.

8 Mimi Swartz and Sherron Watkins (2004), *Power Failure*, p. 225.

9 Phillips, op. cit., p. 169.

10 Sidney Blumenthal (2003), op. cit., p. 739, wrote how Gore felt he could assume the key opinion leaders in DC would be convinced of his integrity.

11 Randal C. Archbold, 'Gore Denies Plans for '04 and Assails Bush Integrity', *New York Times*, 7 August 2003, www.nytimes.com /2003/08/07/politics/gore-denies-plans-for-04-and-assails-bush -integrity/html

12 Quoted in Carl Hulse and David E. Sanger, 'New Criticism on Prewar Use of Intelligence' https://www.nytimes.com/2003/ 09/29/world/new-criticism-on-prewar-use-of-intelligence/html

13 https://www.nytimes.com/2003/08/27/us/in-a-long-presiden tial-race-dean-sprints.html/ But integrity would not go away. And, to one reader, Maureen Labenski, writing a letter to the *New York Times* (Maureen Labenski, 2 September 2003), Dean looked like a winner because he showed the qualities of 'honesty and integrity' that were needed in a leader.

14 David Brooks, 'My Crossover Vote', *New York Times*, 17 January 2004, www.nytimes.com/2004/01/17/opinion/my-crossover-vote/html

15 Paul Krugman, 'Where's the Apology?', *New York Times*, 30 January 2004, online edition, https://www.nytimes.com/2004 /01/30/opinion/where-s-the-apology.html

16 White House press release.

17 Leon Wieseltier, 'Washington Diarist: Against Integrity', *The New Republic*, 24 September 2008 (URL no longer available).

The reference cited here is for a print copy of an online version accessed by this writer on 09 September 2008. The columnist Ramesh Ponnuru commented on the substance of that version in 'Wieseltier on Palin', https://www.nationalreview.com/corner /wieseltier-palin-ramesh-ponnuru/ 11 September, 2008).

18 Ibid.

19 London *Evening Standard* newspaper, 31 August 2022, p. 3.This sense of a completeness to a person's integrity, irrespective of its qualities, echoes an episode John Stuart Mill describes in his *Autobiography* (1924 [1873]), p. 149, where he was building a friendship with Thomas Carlyle. They differed profoundly in their philosophies. Mill writes: 'He soon found out I was not "another mystic", and . . . for the sake of my own integrity I wrote to him a distinct profession of all those opinions which I knew he most disliked . . .'

20 https://www.the guardian.com/comment is free/2021/May/12/ the-guardian-view-on-the-voter-id-bill-cynical-and-hypocritical

21 *The Times*, 'Boyhood fixation with chaos foretold downfall', 9 July 2022, p. 12.

22 Ibid.

23 Reports on the Hutton Inquiry by Nigel Morris, *The Independent*, 19 August 2003, p. 4.

24 BBC television broadcast at 4 pm on 27 May 2021.

25 https://www.the guardian.com/politics/2021/apr/24/boris-john son-a-vacuum-of-integrity-dominic-grieve-joins-downing-stre et-row

26 Edward Luce, 'US media are still Trump's unwitting allies', *Financial Times*, 6 April 2023, p. 24.

Chapter 8 The Integrity Crisis of Our Time

1 Max Weber's account of rationalization as a relentless over-arching process of worldwide social change generalized from the widespread unrelated uses of the term in his time, from American industrial production methods to its use in the new psychoanalytic movement, with both of which he engaged in

depth. His extension of the term to cover the elaboration of religious doctrines over the centuries must count as one of the most imaginative conceptual leaps in the social sciences.

2 See Martin Albrow (1970), *Bureaucracy*.
3 It was these developments that encouraged Talcott Parsons to claim that Herbert Spencer's approach to integration was long outdated.
4 Stuart Chase (1938), 'The Luxury of Integrity', in Irving H. White (ed.), *Essays in Value*, pp. 303-17, p. 304 (published originally in *Harper's Magazine*, 1930).
5 Ibid., p. 315.
6 Ibid., p. 304.
7 David Riesman, (1950), *The Lonely Crowd*; C. Wright Mills (1951), *White Collar*; William H. Whyte (1956), *The Organization Man*. Whyte cited (p. 37) Chase's book, *The Proper Study of Mankind* (1948), for a good description of the human relations school of thought at Harvard Business School.
8 Philip Selznick (1949), *TVA and the Grass Roots*.
9 See Philip Selznick (1957), *Leadership in Administration: A Sociological Interpretation*, pp. 42-9.
10 Philip Selznick (1952), *The Organizational Weapon*.
11 In his study of leadership, after considering the Communist Party, there was no limit to his intellectual ambition, and Selznick went on to compare it with the Department of State as a psychological warfare agency, with the National Association for the Advancement of Colored People and with the retailer Sears, Roebuck. In all cases, he identified values as key to the character definition of the organization (Selznick 1949, pp. 49-56). These days, this is more generally referred to as the USP (unique selling point). That in itself is an indication of commercialization as a societal-wide process.
12 Selznick (1949), p. 130.
13 Ibid., p. 128.
14 Stanley Fish (2008) *Save the World in Your Own Time*, p. 35.
15 Ibid., p. 37.

16 Mimi Swartz and Sherron Watkins (2004), *Power Failure: The Inside Story of the Collapse of Enron*, p. 118.

17 *The New York Times*, 16 January 2002, p. C6.

18 Ibid.

19 Ibid.

20 Ibid., p. C8.

21 *Financial Times Weekend*, 4/5 July 2020, p. 9.

22 Ibid.

23 *Financial Times Weekend Magazine*, 5/6 September 2020, p. 16.

24 *Financial Times*, 'EY abandons appeal against unprecedented sanctions over Wirecard work', 27 March 2024.

25 *Financial Times*, 'EY accused of asset stripping in Wirecard damages case', 9 April 2024.

26 Ibid., 27 September 2023, p. 1.

27 *Financial Times*, 6/7 April 2024, 'Wirecard fugitive faces super-spy allegations', p. 4.

28 https://epa.gov/vw/forms/contact-us-about-volkswagen-violations. For a detailed report and timeline of so-called Dieselgate, see en.m.wikipedia 'Volkswagen Emissions Scandal'.

29 For examples of the unremitting pursuit by the Post Office of the innocent victims of the Horizon software, see *Private Eye* 1615, 10 January/1 February 2024, *Post Office Robbery*.

30 The new director of the Serious Fraud Office, Nick Ephgrave, has suggested consideration might be given to paying whistle-blowers and cites the United States as a place that attracts them from the United Kingdom. He quotes a figure of 700 UK nationals travelling to the United States to blow the whistle because it is so difficult in their own country. 'Pay whistle-blowers to speed up cases', by Bianca Castro, *The Law Society Gazette*, 14 February 2024.

31 David Runciman (2023), *The Handover*, p. 182.

32 Ibid., p. 207. Runciman's speculations end by noting the existential risks confronting humankind, and the autonomy of artificial intelligence (AI) is the latest to appear. It leads him to conclude there are only three choices to be made: bring human intelli-

gence together with AI, e.g., by activating the wisdom of crowds through referenda; allow states to control AI; bring the state together with human intelligence (ibid., p. 271). That last alternative seems to have found a way of precluding AI from securing autonomy, but the way remains obscure.

33 John Bowers (2024), *Downward Spiral*, p. 7.

34 Ibid., p. 8.

35 Bowers (ibid., pp. 226–30) lists fourteen cases that he personally examined, some of which have never received publicity.

36 Kurt Schacht, 'A Network of Insiders', 30 November 2010. http://blogs.cfainstitute.org/marketintegrity/20/11/30/a-net work-of-insiders

37 Frank Zhang and Stuart Baden Powell, 'The Impact of High-Frequency Trading on Markets', *CFA Magazine*, March/April 2011, https://www.cfainstitute.org/-/media/documents/article /cfa-magazine/2011/cfm-v22-n2-3.pdf

38 Robert J. Shiller (2000), *Irrational Exuberance*. Shiller's impressive coverage included a whole range of factors from generational shifts, media impact, foreign investors, Ponzi schemes, 'revealed government corruption' – even the Zeitgeist. Of integrity was there no mention, nor indeed of regulation in general. There may be a good reason. Could it just be that markets are essentially beyond integrity?

39 Adam Smith (1868 [1776]), *The Wealth of Nations*, p. 6.

40 Hernando de Soto (2000), *The Mystery of Capital*.

41 For instance, the new US Corporate Transparency Act aims to bring into the open the beneficial ownership of corporate entities. It does this by requiring professionals like lawyers and accountants to disclose who they work for. Jamie Schafer has pointed to the consequences for these providers of corporate services ('Gatekeepers beware the game-changing US Corporate Transparency Act', *Financial Times*, 19 December 2023, p. 23).

42 Niklas Luhmann wrote extensively and famously from personal training and experience of the way law works and inherently

seeks to define itself as a distinct sphere of society. At no point, however, does he construe this as a search for integrity, even though the concept fits his concerns for the autonomy of law as a system so precisely. Possibly, just speculating, it did not occur to him because he wrote in German, and *integrität* is clearly a loan word. See *A Sociological Theory of Law* (1985); *Law as a Social System* (2004).

43 *Daily Mail*, 'Enemies of the People', 4 November 2016, p. 1.

44 *i* newspaper, 25 January 2017, p. 7.

45 The oligarchs have also found the British legal system useful when they have disputes between themselves. Two of the richest, Oleg Berezovsky and Roman Abramovich, fought a case about their share of assets acquired in the Russian free-for-all in the 1990s, and when it ended in August 2012, they had spent £100 million in legal costs.

46 *Financial Times*, 'Exporting Integrity', 31 August 2012, https://www.ft.com/content/08210afe-f360-11e1-9c6c-00144feabdc0

47 Three cases were referred to the UK Court of Appeal in 2011 on the grounds that a member of a jury had been found guilty of contempt of court and jailed for eight months for expressing sympathy with a defendant in a drugs case and wishing her well. The juror was the first in the United Kingdom to be prosecuted for using the internet during a trial. The Lord Chief Justice declared: 'In the context of current technology, we must be astute to preserve the integrity of the jury trial and the jury system. Modern technology does not come without risks.' MSN News 'Internet "Threat" to Jury Integrity', *The Standard*, 12 April 2012, https://www.standard.co.uk/news/uk/internet-threat-to-jury-integrity-6376807.html

48 The distinction between personal and institutional integrity is clearly expressed in Nicholas Allen and Sarah Birch (2015), *Ethics and Integrity in British Life*, p. 19: 'the overall integrity of a democratic system rests on the integrity of its principal institutions. Politicians should thus ensure that their own conduct does not undermine the integrity of the institution in which they

work.' They draw on Dennis F. Thompson (1987), *Political Ethics and Public Office.*

49 With photographs of many of the signatories, the letter took up the two centre pages of an issue of the *Guardian* newspaper under the heading 'A stand for democracy in the digital age', 10 December 2013, pp. 28–9.

50 Shoshana Zuboff (2019), *The Age of Surveillance Capitalism: The Fight for a Human Future and the New Frontier of Power*, p. 19.

51 For an account of the impact of the media on politics, see J. Street (1997), *Politics and Popular Culture*, and (2001), *Mass Media, Politics and Democracy.* Street advanced the concept of the 'celebrity politician'. See also Neil Washbourne, *Mediating Politics*, 2010, pp. 43–5.

52 *Financial Times*, 'Could theatre be the future of investigative journalism?' by Sam Jones, p. 20, 26 March 2024. Jones makes no mention of the ITV drama, *Mr Bates vs The Post Office*, screened 1–4 January, 2024, but it bears out his point entirely.

Conclusion: Integrity for the Human Future

1 See chapter 7, section entitled 'The British Integrity Vacuum'.

2 Oswald Spengler (2020 [1918/1922]), *The Decline of the West* [*Der Untergang des Abendlandes*].

3 Arnold Toynbee (1934–61), *A Study of History*, 12 vols, Vol. 12, p. 674.

4 Alvin Toffler (1981), *The Third Wave*, p. 305.

5 We can leave to one side a postmodern view that the West has never existed. A division between West and East in Europe developed as the authorities of Rome and Byzantium grew further apart from the fifth century onwards. The Latinate areas came increasingly to be regarded as western. In his *Leviathan*, Thomas Hobbes wrote easily of 'these western parts' being made to receive opinions from Greek and Latin authors (1955 [1651], pp. 140–1).

6 'Unwinding' is also used as a book title in George Packer, *The Unwinding*, 2013. It carries the subtitle 'Thirty Years of American

Decline', and his analogy is the unwinding of a watch. What I want to convey with 'unwinding' is rendered more expressively in the German *Abwickeln*, where there is buried an old image of a bound-up sheaf of corn in a field, ready to be untied. The *Abwicklung* of the West is work in progress. By extension, it has also come to mean the settling of business.

7 No one thinks now of printing or gunpowder coming from China: but they were both invented there.

8 John Locke (1961 [1690]), *An Essay Concerning Human Understanding*, Vol. 2, pp. 36–7. He pointed out that even words for time and weight in Latin seem to offer easy translation into English but in their practical applications in their time they differed very much in their connotations.

9 It took a strange genius nineteen centuries later, Lewis Carroll, to coin a term for a word with two meanings. The context was the poem 'Jabberwocky' in his book *Through the Looking-Glass*, where Alice wanted to know the meaning of 'Twas brillig, and the slithy toves, Did gyre and gimble in the wabe'. Humpty Dumpty explained: 'Well "slithy" means "lithe and slimy". "Lithe" is the same as "active". You see it's like a portmanteau – there are two meanings packed up into one word.' Lewis Carroll (1908 [1871]), p. 128.

10 See Raymond Williams (2014 [1976]), 'Culture', in *Keywords*, pp. 84–90.

11 Locke, op. cit., Vol. I, pp. 25–6.

12 In the past, the idea of a spirit of the age was a frequently used expression, but the rapidity of change today makes it more difficult to fix on any abiding characteristics of the time in which we live. The need to refer to what holds together the time in which we live remains. Cf. ch 7, n 1.

13 'Global culture' is best employed referring to ideas, practices and institutions that relate to the present condition and future of the planet and its inhabitants. Friends of the Earth belongs to global culture. Coca-Cola belongs to world culture, however much it seeks to promote global concerns as part of its image.

14 See ch. 1, pp. 8–9, for Fernand Braudel's emphasis on the importance of Christianity in the development of the West.

15 Thomas Carlyle (1904 [1841]), *On Heroes and Hero-Worship*, p. 162. Significantly, his account of heroes attributed integrity to one only, namely Martin Luther, who sparked off the Reformation. 'A true Great Man; great in intellect, in courage, affection and integrity' (p. 187).

16 By that, I mean my lifetime! Let's rather say since the Second World War.

17 Richard Sennett (1993 [1977]), *The Fall of Public Man*, p. 287. The use of the quotation marks around integrity signal the implausibility of the claim. Sennett uses the example of Richard Nixon to press home his point that diverting the public to focus on the trivia in his motives ('a man who loved dogs') allowed him to avoid examination of his 'slush fund' (ibid., p. 280).

18 Google search, 15 February 2024.

19 It therefore long pre-dates the rise of the concepts that Raymond Williams (1961) identified as finding new meaning at the end of the eighteenth century: industry, democracy, class, art and culture. (*Culture and Society* 1780–1950, p. 13.) But this book is entirely consistent with Williams's approach to finding history inscribed in linguistic innovation.

20 I made a similar point some time ago (perhaps over-optimistically!): 'The professional official has achieved emancipation from the machine to follow the objectives of his professional conscience' (Albrow 1971, 'Public Administration and Sociological Theory', p. 356).

21 For theoretical insight, see above, chapter 4, for the 'pure relationship' (Giddens 1991, 1992).

22 Leonard Woolf (1928), *Imperialism and Civilization*, p. 7.

23 Ibid., p. 133. There are many ironies here. He was the husband of Virginia Woolf, queen of that rather precious group we met in chapter 5, the Bloomsberries. There is little, if any, evidence that she was interested in his political work, or indeed his book.

References

Acton, Lord (1891) 'Introduction' to *Il Principe* by Niccolo Machiavelli, ed. L. Arthur Bird. Oxford: Clarendon Press.

Acton, Lord (ed.) (1902–10) *Cambridge Modern History*. 12 vols. Cambridge: Cambridge University Press.

Albrow, Martin (1970) *Bureaucracy*. London: Pall Mall Press.

Albrow, Martin (1971) 'Public Administration and Sociological Theory', *Advancement of Science* 27(134): 347–56.

Albrow, Martin (1996) *The Global Age: State and Society beyond Modernity*. Cambridge: Polity.

Albrow, Martin (2014a) *Global Age Essays on Social and Cultural Change*. Frankfurt am Main: Vittorio Klostermann.

Albrow, Martin (2014b) 'Local Integrities and Global Interconnectedness', in M. Albrow, *Global Age Essays on Social and Cultural Change*, pp. 127–37.

Albrow, Martin (2021) *China and the Shared Human Future: Exploring Common Values and Goals*, ed. Xiangqun Chang. London: Global Century Press.

Albrow, Martin and Wei, JIN (2021) 'Spirit (精神 *jingshen*) as a Key Contemporary Chinese Concept', *Journal of China in Global and Comparative Perspective* 7.

Allen, Nicholas and Birch, Sarah (2015) *Ethics and Integrity in British Life*. Cambridge: Cambridge University Press.

Anderson, Lee F. (1968) 'Education and Social Science in the Context of an Emerging Global Society', in James M. Becker and Howard D. Mehlinger (eds), *International Dimensions in the Social* Studies, 38th Yearbook. Washington, DC: National Council for the Social Studies, pp. 78–98.

Angell, Robert C. (1941) *The Integration of American Society*. New York: McGraw Hill.

Annan, Noel (1990) *Our Age: Portrait of a Generation*. London: Weidenfeld and Nicolson.

Aquinas, Thomas (1954) *Selected Political Writings*, ed. A. P. D'Entreves, trans. J. G Dawson. Oxford: Blackwell.

Arendt, Hannah (1998 [1958]) *The Human Condition*. Chicago: University of Chicago Press.

Austen, Jane (1980 [1814]) *Mansfield Park*. Oxford: Oxford University Press.

Bacon, Francis (2002) *The Major Works*, ed. Brian Vickers. Oxford: Oxford University Press.

Bacon, Francis (2002 [1605]) *The Advancement of Learning*, in *The Major Works*, ed. Brian Vickers. Oxford: Oxford University Press, pp. 120–299.

Bacon, Francis (2002 [1626]) *The New Atlantis* in *The Major Works*, ed. Brian Vickers. Oxford: Oxford University Press, pp. 457–89.

Bell, Clive (1928) *Civilization: An Essay*. London: Chatto and Windus.

Bell, Clive (1988 [1956]) *Old Friends*. London: Cassell.

Bell, Daniel (1980) *The Winding Passage: Essays and Sociological Journeys 1960–1980*. New York: Basic Books.

Bennett, William J. (1997) *The Spirit of America*. New York: Touchstone.

Bible, The Holy (1611) King James Version. London: Robert Barker.

Blumenthal, Sidney (2003) *The Clinton Wars*. New York: Farrar, Straus and Giroux.

Boswell, James (1906 [1791]) *The Life of Dr Johnson*. London: Dent Everyman.

Bowers, John (2024) *Downward Spiral: Collapsing Public Standards and How to Restore Them.* Manchester: Manchester University Press.

Braudel, Fernand (1995 [1963]) *A History of Civilizations*, trans. Richard Mayne. Harmondsworth: Penguin.

Burns, Tom (1992) *Erving Goffman.* London: Routledge.

Bush, George H. W. (1988) *George Bush: Man of Integrity.* Eugene, OR: Harvest House.

Capra, Fritjof (1976) *The Tao of Physics.* London: Fontana,

Carlyle, Thomas (1904 [1841]) *On Heroes, Hero-Worship and the Heroic in History.* London: Oxford University Press.

Carroll, Lewis (1908 [1871]) *Through the Looking-Glass and What Alice Found There.* London: Macmillan.

Carter, Stephen L. (1996) *Integrity.* New York: HarperPerennial.

Channing. W. E. (1870) *The Complete Works.* London: George Routledge.

Chase, Stuart (1938) 'The Luxury of Integrity', in Irving H. White (ed.), *Essays in Value.* London and New York: D. Appleton Century.

Chase, Stuart (1948) *The Proper Study of Mankind.* New York: Harper & Brothers.

Cicero, Marcus Tullius (1939 [1st cent. BCE]) *Brutus Orator*, trans. G. L. Hendrickson and H. M. Hubbell. Cambridge, MA: Harvard University Press.

Cockell, Charles (2019) *The Equations of Life: How Physics Shapes Evolution.* London: Atlantic Books.

Confucius (1979 [5th cent. BCE]) *The Analects*, trans. D. C. Lau. Harmondsworth: Penguin.

Driberg, Tom (1978) *Ruling Passions.* London: Jonathan Cape.

Dworkin, Ronald (1985) *A Matter of Principle.* Cambridge, MA: Harvard University Press.

Eliade, Mircea (1954) *The Myth of the Eternal Return, or Cosmos and History.* New York: Princeton University Press.

Feng Youlan (1939) *Xin yuan ren* [A New Treatise on the Nature of Man]. Chongqing: Commercial Press.

Fish, Stanley (2008) *Save the World on Your Own Time*. New York: Oxford University Press.

Franklin, Benjamin (1793) *Autobiography*, in J. A. L. Lemay and P. M. Zall (eds), *Benjamin Franklin's Autobiography*. New York: W. W. Norton.

Friedman, Thomas L. (1999) *The Lexus and the Olive Tree*. New York: Farrar, Straus, Giroux.

Fromm, Erich (1942) *The Fear of Freedom*. London: Routledge & Kegan Paul.

Fromm, Erich (1956) *The Sane Society*. London: Routledge & Kegan Paul.

Fromm, Erich (1957) *The Art of Loving*. London: Unwin.

Giddens, Anthony (1991) *Modernity and Self Identity: Self and Society in the Late Modern Age*. Cambridge: Polity.

Giddens, Anthony (1992) *The Transformation of Intimacy: Sexuality, Love and Eroticism in Modern Societies*. Cambridge: Polity.

Goffman, Erving (1967) *Interaction Ritual: Essays on Face-to-Face Behavior*. New York: Anchor Books.

Goffman, Erving (1968) *Asylums: Essays on the Social Situation of Mental Patients and Other Inmates*. Harmondsworth: Penguin.

Goffman, Erving (1968) *Stigma: Notes on the Management of Spoiled Identity*. Harmondsworth: Penguin.

Goffman, Erving (1971) *Relations in Public: Microstudies of the Public Order*. Harmondsworth: Penguin.

Goffman, Erving (1971 [1959]) *The Presentation of Self in Everyday Life*. Harmondsworth: Penguin.

Goffman, Erving (1975) *Frame Analysis: An Essay on the Organization of Experience*. Harmondsworth: Penguin.

Goffman, Erving (1981) *Forms of Talk*. Oxford: Blackwell.

Goodman, Paul (1960) *Growing up Absurd*. New York: Vintage Books.

Gore, Al (1992) *Earth in the Balance: Ecology and the Human Spirit*. Boston: Houghton Mifflin.

Grand Larousse de la Langue Française (1975). Paris: Librairie Larousse.

Greenblatt, Stephen (2012) *The Swerve: How the Renaissance Began*. London: Vintage.

Griffith, Jeremy (1988) *Free: The End of the Human Condition*. Sydney: Centre for Humanity's Adulthood.

Groot, J. J. M. de (1918) *Universismus: Die Grundlage der Religion und Ethik, des Staatswesens und der Wissenschaften Chinas*. Berlin: Georg Reimer.

Halmos, Paul (1970) *The Personal Service Society*. London: Constable.

Hassall, A. (1926 [1749]) *Bolingbroke on the Spirit of Patriotism and on the Idea of a Patriot King*. Oxford: Clarendon Press.

Hawthorne, Nathaniel (2000 [1850]) *The Scarlet Letter*. New York: Modern Library.

Hegel, G. W. F. (1931 [1807]) *The Phenomenology of Mind*, trans. J. B. Baillie. London: George Allen & Unwin.

Hewitt, Rachel (2017) *A Revolution of Feeling: The Decade that Forged the Modern Mind*. London: Granta.

Hobbes, Thomas (1955 [1651]) *Leviathan*. Oxford: Blackwell.

Hodgson, Anthony (2019) *Systems Thinking for a Turbulent World: A Search for New Perspectives*. Abingdon: Routledge.

Holmes, Richard (2008) *The Age of Wonder: How the Romantic Generation Discovered the Beauty and Terror of Science*. London: Harper Collins.

Jardine, Lisa and Stewart, Alan (1999) *Hostage to Fortune: The Troubled Life of Francis Bacon 1561–1626*. London: Phoenix.

Johnson, Samuel (1825 [1785]) *A Dictionary of the English Language*, 6th edn. Vol. 1. London: Rivington.

Johnson, Samuel (1825) *The Works of Samuel Johnson*, 9 vols. London: Tallboys and Wheeler and W. Pickering. Vol. 1, pp. 386–9.

Johnson, Samuel (1975 [1759]) *Rasselas*. London: Folio Society.

Johnston, Arthur (ed.) (1965) *Francis Bacon*. London: Batsford.

Julian of Norwich (1966 [*c.* 1323]) *Revelations of Divine Love*, ed. Clifton Wolters. London: Penguin.

Kalberg, Stephen (2014) *Searching for the Spirit of American Democracy: Max Weber's Analysis of a Unique Political Culture, Past, Present, and Future*. Boulder, CO: Paradigm.

Kerouac, Jack (1957) *On the Road*. New York: Viking.

Klein, Melanie (1975) *The Collected Writing*s, 4 vols. London: Hogarth Press.

Koestler, Arthur (1970) *The Ghost in the Machine*. London: Pan.

Kwarteng, Kwasi (2011) *Ghosts of Empire: Britain's Legacies in the Modern World*. London: Bloomsbury.

Lao Zi (2013 [5th cent. BCE]) *The Collected Works of Ancient Chinese Philosophy: Lao Zi Says*. Beijing: Sinolingua.

Larkin, Philip (1988) *Collected Poems*. London: Faber and Faber.

Lawrence, D. H. (1923) *Studies in Classic American Literature*. New York: T. Seltzer.

Leicester, Graham (2016) *Transformative Innovation*. Axminster: Triarchy.

Lemay, J. A. Leo and Zall, P. M. (eds) (1986 [1793]) *Benjamin Franklin's Autobiography*. New York: W. W. Norton.

Levitt, Theodore (1983) 'The Globalization of Markets'. *Harvard Business Review*, May–June: 92–102.

Locke, John (1961 [1690]) *An Essay Concerning Human Understanding*, 2 vols. London: J. M. Dent.

Lockwood, David (1964) 'Social Integration and System Integration', in Z. Zollschan and W. Hirsch (eds), *Explorations in Social Change*. London: Routledge and Kegan Paul.

Lovelock, James (1988) *The Age of Gaia*. New York: W. W. Norton.

Lucretius (1982) *On the Nature of Things [De Rerum Naturae]*, trans. W. H. D. Rouse, rev. Martin F. Smith. Cambridge, MA: Harvard University Press, Loeb Classical Library.

Lugard, Lord (1925) 'Education in Tropical Africa', *Edinburgh Review* (July): 2–9.

Luhmann, Niklas (1985) *A Sociological Theory of Law*, trans. Elizabeth King-Utz and Martin Albrow. London: Routledge and Kegan Paul.

Luhmann, Niklas (2004) *Law as a Social System*, trans. Klaus A. Ziegert. Oxford: Oxford University Press.

MacGregor, James and Dunn, Susan (2001) *The Three Roosevelts: Patrician Leaders Who Transformed America*. New York: Atlantic Monthly Press.

Machiavelli, Niccolo (1903 [1513]) *The Prince*, trans. Luigi Ricci. London: Henry Frowde.

MacIntyre, Alasdair (1985) *After Virtue: A Study in Moral Theory*. London: Duckworth.

Madge, Charles (1964) *Society in the Mind: Elements of Social Eidos*. London: Faber and Faber.

Mandeville, Bernard (1989 [1724]) *The Fable of the Bees*, ed. P. Harth. London: Penguin.

Margulis, Lynn (1993) *Symbiosis in Cell Evolution*. New York: Freeman.

Marx, Karl (1973) *Grundrisse*, trans. Martin Nicolaus. Harmondsworth: Penguin.

Marx, Karl and Engels, Frederick (1977) *Collected Works, Volume 9: Marx and Engels: 1849*. London: Lawrence and Wishart.

Maturana, Humberto R. and Varela, Francisco J. (1981) *Autopoiesis and Cognition: The Realization of the Living*. Boston: D. Reidel.

McGilchrist, Iain (2009) *The Master and His Emissary: The Divided Brain and the Making of the Western World*. New Haven: Yale University Press.

Mead, George H. (1934) *Mind, Self and Society*, 3 vols. Chicago: Chicago University Press.

Merleau-Ponty, Maurice (1973) *The Prose of the World*. Evanston, IL: Northwestern University Press.

Middle English Dictionary (1968), ed. Sherman M. Kuhn and John Reedy. Ann Arbor, MI: University of Michigan Press.

Mill, John Stuart (1924 [1873]) *Autobiography*. London: Oxford University Press.

Mills, C. Wright (1956) *White Collar*. New York: Oxford University Press.

Mohrmann. Margaret E. (2004) 'Integrity: Integritas, Innocentia, Simplicitas', *Journal of the Society of Christian Ethics* 24(2): 25-37.

Montaigne, Michel de (1842 [1588]) 'Of Presumption', in *The Works of Montaigne*, ed. and trans. William Hazlitt. London: John Templeman.

Munsterberg, Hugo (1904) *The Americans*. New York: McClure, Phillips.

Needham, Joseph (1969) *The Grand Titration: Science and Society in East and West*. London: Allen & Unwin.

Nietzsche, Friedrich (1969 [1889] *Twilight of the Idols and the Antichrist*, trans. R. J. Hollingdale. Harmondsworth: Penguin.

O'Neill, Nena and O'Neill, George (1973) *Open Marriage: A New Lifestyle for Couples*. New York: Avon.

Orwell, George (1937) *The Road to Wigan Pier*. London: Victor Gollancz.

Orwell, George (1945) *Animal Farm: A Fairy Story*. London: Secker and Warburg.

Oxford English Dictionary (Compact Edition) (1971). Oxford: Clarendon Press.

Oxford Latin Dictionary (1982). Oxford: Clarendon Press.

Packer, George (2013) *The Unwinding: Thirty Years of American Decline*. London: Faber & Faber.

Parsons, Talcott (1951) *The Social System*. London: Routledge & Kegan Paul.

Parsons, Talcott (1953) 'The Theory of Symbolism in Relation to Action', in Talcott Parsons, R. F. Bales and E. A. Shils, *Working Papers in the Theory of Action*. New York: The Free Press.

Parsons, Talcott (1954) *Essays in Sociological Theory*. Glencoe, IL: The Free Press.

Parsons, Talcott and Shils, E. A. (eds) (1962) *Toward a General Theory of Action*. New York: Harper.

Parsons, Talcott, Bales, R. F. and Shils, E. A. (1953) *Working Papers in the Theory of Action*. New York: The Free Press.

Partridge, Frances (1981) *Memories*. London: Gollancz.

Peel, J. D. Y. (1971) *Herbert Spencer: The Evolution of a Sociologist*. London: Heinemann.

Phillips, Kevin (2004) *American Dynasty: Aristocracy, Fortune, and the Politics of Deceit in the House of Bush*. New York: Penguin.

Pirsig, Robert (1974) *Zen and the Art of Motorcycle Maintenance: An Inquiry into Values*. New York: William Morrow.

Radin, Paul (1957 [1927]) *Primitive Man as Philosopher*. New York: Dover.

Rawls, John (1999 [1971]) *A Theory of Justice*. Cambridge, MA: Harvard University Press.

Riesman, David (1950) *The Lonely Crowd: A Study of the Changing American Character*. New Haven: Yale University Press.

Runciman, David (2023) *The Handover: How We Gave Control of Our Lives to Corporations, States and AIs*. London: Profile.

Russell, Bertrand (1938) *Power: A New Social Analysis*. London: George Allen & Unwin.

Russell, Bertrand (1945) *A History of Western Philosophy*. New York: Simon and Schuster.

Ryle, Gilbert (1949) *The Concept of Mind*. London: Hutchinson.

Sackville-West, Vita (1930) *The Edwardians*. London: Hogarth Press.

Said, Edward W. (1994) *Culture and Imperialism*. London: Vintage Books.

Sartre, Jean-Paul (1988 [1953]) *Being and Nothingness: An Essay on Phenomenological Ontology*. London: Heinemann.

Selznick, Philip (1949) *TVA and the Grass Roots*. Berkeley and Los Angeles: University of California Press.

Selznick, Philip (1952) *The Organizational Weapon*. New York: McGraw Hill.

Selznick, Philip (1957) *Leadership in Administration: A Sociological Interpretation*. New York: Harper & Row.

Sennett, Richard (1993 [1977]) *The Fall of Public Man*. London and Boston: Faber and Faber.

Shiller, Robert J. (2000) *Irrational Exuberance*. Princeton, NJ: Princeton University Press.

Smith, Adam (1868 [1776]) *An Inquiry into the Nature and Causes of the Wealth of Nations*. London: Nelson.

Solint, Rebecca (2021) *Orwell's Roses*. London: Granta.

Soto, Hernando de (2000) *The Mystery of Capital*. New York: Basic Books.

Spencer, Herbert (1910 [1862]) *First Principles*, Vol. 2. London: Williams and Norgate.

Spender, Matthew (2015) *A House in St John's Wood: In Search of My Parents*. London: HarperCollins.

Spender, Stephen (1951) *World within World*. London: Hamish Hamilton.

Spender, Stephen (1969) *The Year of the Young Rebels*. New York: Vintage Books.

Spengler, Oswald (1926 [1920/22]) *The Decline of the West* (*Der Untergang des Abendlandes*), trans. Charles Francis Atkinson. London: George Allen & Unwin.

Street, John (1997) *Politics and Popular Culture*. Cambridge: Polity.

Street, John (2001) *Mass Media, Politics and Democracy*. Houndmills: Palgrave.

Sumner, William Graham (1919) *The Forgotten Man and Other Essays*, ed. A. G. Keller. New Haven: Yale University Press.

Swartz, Mimi and Watkins, Sherron (2004) *Power Failure: The Inside Story of the Collapse of Enron*. New York: Doubleday.

Taylor, Charles (1975) *Hegel*. Cambridge: Cambridge University Press.

Thompson, Dennis F. (1987) *Political Ethics and Public Office*. Cambridge, MA: Harvard University Press.

Tocqueville, Alexis de (1994 [1835–40]) *Democracy in America*, ed. J. P. Mayer. London: Fontana.

Toffler, Alvin (1981) *The Third Wave*. London: Pan.

Toynbee, Arnold (1961) *A Study of History*, Vol. XII. London: Oxford University Press.

Waldman, Michael (2000) *Potus Speaks*. New York: Simon and Schuster.

Wang Yiwei (2016) *The Belt and Road Initiative: What Will China Offer to the World in Its Rise*. Beijing: New World Press.

Washbourne, Neil (2010) *Mediating Politics: Newspapers, Radio, Television and the Internet*. Maidenhead: Open University Press.

Weber, Marianne (1974 [1926]) *Max Weber: A Biography*, trans. Harry Zohn. New York: John Wiley.

Weber, Max (2009 [1920]) *The Protestant Ethic and the Spirit of Capitalism with Other Writings on the Rise of the West*, trans. Stephen Kalberg. Oxford: Oxford University Press.

Welsh Academy English–Welsh Dictionary (1995). Cardiff: University of Wales Press.

Welsh Language, Dictionary of the (2014) GPC online. https://www.welsh-dictionary.ac.uk

Wheen, Francis (1990) *Tom Driberg: His Life and Indiscretions.* London: Chatto and Windus.

White, Irving H. (ed.) (1938) *Essays in Value.* London and New York: D. Appleton Century.

Whyte, William H. (1956) *The Organization Man.* New York: Simon and Schuster.

Wieseltier, Leon (2008), 'Against Integrity', *The New Republic*, 24 September.

Wikipedia. 'Grover Cleveland', updated 23 October 2020.

Williams, Bernard (2002) *Truth and Truthfulness: An Essay in Genealogy.* Princeton: Princeton University Press.

Williams, Raymond (1961) *Culture and Society 1780–1950.* Harmondsworth: Penguin.

Williams, Raymond (2014 [1976]) *Keywords.* London: Fourth Estate.

Williams Jr, Robin M. (1966) *American Society: A Sociological Interpretation.* New York: Knopf.

Williams, Jennifer (n.d.) *Common Threads for Uncommon People.* London: Centre for Creative Communities.

Woolf, Leonard (1928) *Imperialism and Civilization.* London: Hogarth Press.

Wordsworth, William (1971) *The Prelude*, ed. J. C. Maxwell. Harmondsworth: Penguin.

Wrong, Dennis H. (1961) 'The Over-Socialized Conception of Man in Modern Sociology', *American Sociological Review* 26(2): 183–93.

Xi Jinping (2014) *The Governance of China*, Vol. 1. Beijing: Foreign Languages Press.

Zollschan Z. and Hirsch, W. (eds) (1964) *Explorations in Social Change.* London: Routledge and Kegan Paul.

Zuboff, Shoshana (2019) *The Age of Surveillance Capitalism: The Fight for a Human Future and the New Frontier of Power.* London: Profile Books.

Index